"The book provides concrete action items for solving workplace bullying, all while exploring pros and con.., what's worked and what hasn't, why something is or isn't...The discussio.. .. ..d profou.. .. .. ..on items are definite and ..l.. ..

Cathe .. .. ..oPr .. .. .. *speaker,*
.. ..ant a.. .. *k-A$$*
————— *it Work*

"A wond.......ly refreshing analysis t.. .. phisticated and accessible analysis of healthcare, work relations, .. .d mental health while still managing to retain some optimism about .. .cky task of surviving work."
Melanie Simms, F ..**ssor of Work and Employment, University of Leicester**

"Elizabeth Cotton is an innovative, creative thinker who turns her 'talk' into 'walk'. She has immense experience of listening to and working with front line staff who are trying to grapple with the impact of workplace stress, bullying, harassment and discrimination. She is fortunate to ally that with extensive knowledge of the theory and practice of mental health. We have much to learn from her, not just as individuals seeking to demonstrate resilience in the face of toxic pressures, but in how to develop collective approaches to the challenges we all face at work."
Roger Kline, NHS Workforce Race Equality Standard

"This book is a must for those working in mental health services, either as clinicians or managers. Written by a clinician and trade unionist it provides a unique approach to understanding and addressing the pressures at the front line of care and how to survive in our working environment."
Clare Gerada, Practitioner Health Programme

"If you want to be informed about the general climate of the health and helping professions you could not do better than invest in this new publication. It is based on a wide range of in-depth interviews and research, and will put you fully in the picture of both difficulties and opportunities in this field."
Anton Obholzer, emeritus Chief Executive, Tavistock Centre

"I am forever grateful to Elizabeth Cotton for the oxygen that her thinking and writing delivers. She understands those of us working on the frontline and can say the things we often can't. This book is not just a survival manual for work, it takes us on a personal and relational journey. Food for thought and action."
Chris Manning, Action for NHS Wellbeing

Surviving Work in Healthcare

The book takes as its starting point the crisis of healthcare in the UK: impossible health targets managed through command and control management and a stomach-churning rise in racism, whistleblowing and victimisation in the NHS. The use of nationally set productivity targets combined with austerity cuts have increasingly put clinical best-practice into direct conflict with funding. Health targets have become politically controlled, and performance has become a cynical exercise in ticking boxes, cascaded within trusts and bulldozed through frontline services. This has led directly to a precarious system of employment relations, subject to the continual restructuring of services rather than the goal of creating functioning interdisciplinary teams that stand a chance of capturing clinical excellence.

This book is written for workers and managers who are on the frontline of the battle for decent healthcare. The content of this book is based on the 'ordinary' expertise of the people who are actually surviving it and helpful ideas about making the best out of a bad lot.

Surviving Work in Healthcare will be of interest to healthcare professionals and anyone working on the frontline of healthcare as well as students of management, human resources and psychology.

Dr Elizabeth Cotton is a writer and educator working in the field of mental health at work. She teaches and writes academically about employment relations and precarious work, business and management, adult education, solidarity and team working. Elizabeth worked as an organiser and educator for global trade unions, principally as head of education for Industriall, working with activists from thirty-five developing and transition economies. She has worked as a psychotherapist in the NHS and runs Surviving Work (www.survivingwork.org), a free resource for working people on how to do it. She has recently set up a joint resource with the Tavistock and Portman NHS Foundation Trust for people working on the frontline of healthcare (www.survivingworkinhealth.org) and is currently researching future trends in mental health services and jobs in the UK.

Surviving Work in Healthcare

Helpful stuff for people on the frontline

Elizabeth Cotton

Routledge
Taylor & Francis Group

LONDON AND NEW YORK

First published 2017
by Routledge
2 Park Square, Milton Park, Abingdon, Oxon OX14 4RN

and by Routledge
711 Third Avenue, New York, NY 10017

Routledge is an imprint of the Taylor & Francis Group, an informa business

British Library Cataloguing-in-Publication Data
A catalogue record for this book is available from the British Library

Library of Congress Cataloging-in-Publication Data
Names: Cotton, Elizabeth (Psychotherapist) author.
Title: Surviving work in healthcare : how to manage working in health and
    social care / Elizabeth Cotton.
Description: Milton Park, Abingdon, Oxon ; New York, NY : Routledge,
    2017. | Includes bibliographical references and index.
Identifiers: LCCN 2016041920 | ISBN 9781472464286 (hbk) |
    ISBN 9780415788045 (pbk) | ISBN 9781315611419 (ebk)
Subjects: LCSH: Health care reform—Great Britain. | Medical care—Great
    Britain. | Great Britain. National Health Service. | Transformation. |
    Social service.
Classification: LCC RA395.G6 C668 2017 | DDC 362.10941–dc23
LC record available at https://lccn.loc.gov/2016041920

ISBN: 978-1-4724-6428-6 (hbk)
ISBN: 978-0-415-78804-5 (pbk)
ISBN: 978-1-315-61141-9 (ebk)

Typeset in Bembo
by Apex CoVantage, LLC

For my parents who brought me up to believe that the world should be fair and Fred Higgs who showed me how to fight for it.

Contents

Preface

"Vulnerability has become associated with failure."

This book comes out of five years working with health workers and activists under the title of Surviving Work. This involved running courses and discussion events and weekly blogging on topics ranging from how to tackle bullying at work to whether you need to marry a rich man to be a psychotherapist in the UK.

Just for the record, of the thousands of people working in healthcare whom I have met both in the flesh and virtually, I would be happy for every single one of you to run the NHS.

For the thoughts and ideas you sent in response to the Surviving Work blogs over the years. Thank you. To the psychosocial academics and researchers who reminded me that actual facts matter. Thank you. To the folk who came to our survival events and courses and allowed yourselves to go through the pain threshold of free association on issues that actually matter. Thank you.

In 2016 I carried out a national survey of working conditions of mental health workers in the UK – the results of which can be accessed on www. survivingworksurvey.org. To the 1,500 people working in mental health who took part and talked me through the dilemmas they face every day. Thank you. Despite the profound societal attack on our compassionate hearts, I have been overwhelmed by your love and respect for your patients and the sheer bravery many of you show just by turning up at work each day.

Each chapter starts with an extract from conversations with thinkers and practitioners in healthcare. In 2015 I carried out a series of conversations in partnership with the Tavistock and Portman NHS Trust to develop free materials using psychoanalytic ideas on how to improve working life. The videos, podcasts and guides that were developed for this project can be accessed for free on www.survivingworkinheath.org. To the people who gave their time to have these conversations, wow. Just wow.

In a way this book has taken a lifetime to write because it draws on my experience of working as a trade unionist, an educator and a psychotherapist. The experience of trying to get help through my own analysis, kicking and screaming the entire way, has been a deep and profound learning experience and has shaped the style of the book, which aims to be humane and realistic.

Working in health means walking the thin line between hypocrisy and genuine knowledge. I set up Surviving Work not because I'm good at it but precisely because I'm not. To the people who helped me keep my chin up throughout this process, for what it's worth my humanity is entirely thanks to you.

What I have learned from you does not make me happy or rich, but it does help me survive work.

1 Understanding healthcare systems

"Working in health and social care is a political thing. It doesn't matter what your ideology is, we're dealing with political phenomena like the winding down of the welfare state and the fact that 30% of health workers are also on benefits because they don't earn enough."

Surviving work conversation: understanding healthcare systems

MARIANNA: By systemic change I mean that the discourses and meanings have changed that are associated with health and care. They are concretised by financial arrangements, but actually they are based on political ideologies in my view.

JULIAN: It seems to me that the financial structure that we're now struggling with could never have taken place if the idea of the welfare settlement hadn't been so seriously challenged. The welfare state became renamed 'The Nanny' without asking where the money had gone and why. There's also been the relentless denigration of professionals. So you had an attack on the instruments of welfare – undermining its value as a humane social function – it becomes this endless debate about the destructiveness of dependency. Then you attack the workers – calling them charlatans – and attack them so comprehensively whether they're care workers or social workers. Currently the current junior doctors' contract is a disgrace. I speak with some feeling about it because my daughter is one. It's the relentless substitution of the professional class by the consuming class. The ideological context is just as important as privatisation.

MARIANNA: Vulnerability has been associated with failure. For example if you are sacked from your job you must be doing something wrong. If you are ill it is your personal failure. This is underpinned by attacking anything that is to do with collective values, collective action and just relationality like communities, even families. Your metaphor of the mother and the nanny – a person we normally pay, a person we contract out to provide care, and that shift is so fundamental. It has such a deeper meaning and consequences. On the one hand vulnerability is just exiled, it's a personal failure, and on the other hand those individuals are also consumers. No more citizens or people in need. The concept of being human is just collapsed into a concept of being a consumer.

JULIAN: It's penetrated so much of the training now. The training I had as a social worker – the psychosocial underpinning of it – moving more and more into an instrumental competency-based training in which the relational has taken a very poor second.

MARIANNA: Actually the patient doesn't know why his or her care is the last consideration in the whole system. You have different people who design care, different people who report on financial targets, different people who are on the front line. Nurses versus doctors are endlessly pitted against each other, and the patients' interests are often going out of the window. That splitting is by design – introduced to break down this collective logic that underpins the collective values that in turn underpin the NHS. Universalistic values, this is what's been attacked.

To hear the full conversation between Julian Lousada and Marianna Fotaki go to www.survivingworkinhealth.org.

Understanding healthcare systems

Keeping track of reform in healthcare is literally a full time job. Even senior healthcare professionals struggle to keep up with the daily reports on new policies, funding deficits, Care Quality Commission (CQC) reports, academic research and steady flow of crises in local services. This book was written during the summer of 2016 – holidays being the traditional period of radical cuts and new government policy slipped in while the healthcare leadership are tucked away in the south of France. No trade union can organise a meeting let alone strike action, and urgent emails are returned with auto messages of 'I'm really tired, leave me alone'.

Not wishing to get all conspiratorial on you, but this is pretty convenient for the individuals and organisations that have failed to win the political battle to shut down the NHS but have made enormous progress in dismantling it by stealth.

For many people working in healthcare the bigger picture is a depressingly obscure patchwork of shiny 'new' management techniques, bad news, smoke, mirrors and a sense of déjà vu. On the last day of writing this book I clicked onto Twitter to find the long awaited results of a review of bursaries for midwives and nurses – all gone, replaced by student loans and unconfirmed announcements of a 40% cut in Health Education England's budget. Goodbye to the development of the next generation of frontline health workers without even pause for a headline.

As the proofs came in there was a moment when I thought about putting a match to the whole manuscript because of the emergence of the Sustainability and Transformation Plans (STPs) which, despite their claims to putting power into local hands, represent a catastrophic reduction in funding and clinical decision making in the NHS. Nobody had ever mentioned STPs throughout the whole process of writing this book and yet by December 2016 their introduction by stealth threatens to obliterate what remains of any prospect of managing healthcare.

Campaigning groups that have very quickly mobilised around blocking STPs, such as in Liverpool and Sheffield, estimate that the plans include an implicit target to cut NHS spending by a further £25.5bn. They call them Secret Theft Plans or Slash Trash and Plunder. It is my considered view that public health services in the UK will die out over the next ten years. What is emerging is a downgraded model of sub-care, a regime of compulsory fitness founded on gaming data and demoralised workers. This radical shift towards un-care is welcomed with wide open strategic arms by the thousands of private contractors and employment agencies waiting to negotiate the next round of health contracts. As the great and the good retire and new generations of workers enter a confused market with no sniff of a pension or secure housing, the crisis in health is about to hit a tipping point. This is just my view; I sincerely hope I am wrong.

This book is written with this tipping point in mind, for workers and managers who are on the frontline of the battle for decent healthcare. In order not to add to your problems I have attempted to present a model for understanding and surviving work that does not ask you to risk your own health or sanity. The content of this book is based on the 'ordinary' expertise of the people who are actually surviving it and helpful ideas about making the best out of a bad lot. It is written in a non-academic and at times blunt way, but what it loses in subtlety it gains in authenticity. I believe that organising and psychoanalysis are ordinary processes for ordinary people that can be talked about in ordinary language. So, if you are a political or psychoanalytic purist, this book will annoy you, so save yourself the bother and put it down now.

Surviving work is a dual task – it involves both trying to change our working conditions while at the same time surviving them. Most of us cannot actually afford to lose our jobs, and that is a reality that has to be a part of the survival strategy. The proposals within this book are directed at this dual objective of transformation and survival under current conditions, so using them is not dependent on systemic change or winning the battle for the NHS. You do not need anyone's permission to start to build your relationships at work, and whatever the outcomes of the next few years of reform, these techniques will put you in a good position to survive them.

The proposal that I want to pitch to you in this book goes like this.

From targets to teams

Over the last thirty years of marketisation of public services, the way healthcare is managed has moved away from a focus on delivering services towards a preoccupation with performance management. We have seen the growth of New Public Management (NPM) techniques to address a problem of demand outweighing supply in healthcare by reducing it to a technical problem of staff productivity and efficiencies. In stark contrast to this sanitised picture stand the Francis reports, following the Mid-Staffs inquiries, which offer us an insight into the crisis of care in the UK: impossible health targets managed through command and control management and a stomach-churning rise in racism, whistleblowing and victimisation in the NHS.

The use of nationally set productivity targets combined with austerity cuts have increasingly put clinical best-practice into direct conflict with funding. This has led to a cynical culture of gaming in NHS management – where ticking boxes has become a parallel system of political football. The balls that get kicked around include waiting times in Accident and Emergency (A&E) and 'recovery' rates in mental health which generally involve putting patients in 'holding' positions, where initial contact is made in a relatively quick time but treatment by senior clinicians much further down the line. This is not measuring treatment, it is measuring waiting lists.

In order to prove the efficiency of this new economic logic, the drive to introduce accountability measurements has been intense. Health targets have become politically controlled and centralised, with government ministers dictating what healthcare providers should do and by when, unencumbered by any actual clinical experience or knowledge of the communities where healthcare is being delivered. NHS performance has become a top-down command and control system, cascaded within trusts and bulldozing through frontline services. This has led directly to a chaotic system of employment relations, subject to the continual restructuring of services rather than the goal of creating functioning interdisciplinary teams that stand a chance of capturing clinical excellence. In response to the NHS deficit generated by escalating demand and chronic underfunding of adult social care, in 2014 the Chief Executive of the NHS in England, Simon Stevens proposed proposed A Five Year Forward View which aims to maintain quality services through innovation and cost savings in return for additional governmental funding by 2020–21. Part of this deficit relates to healthcare providers - estimated at £2.45bn - unable to deliver 'efficiencies', particularly in relation to staffing costs and the rising cost of agency labour. A key part of the Five Year Forward plan is the creation of Sustainability and Transformation Plans (STPs), which despite their progressive name stand to be probably the least sustainable plan for NHS restructuring to date.

STPs, clustered in acute and specialist care which represents the main bulk of provider deficit in the NHS, are tasked with eliminating the gap between costs and funding by creating 44 'local health systems' that create 'footprints' for planning and delivering care. If they manage to do this in 2016/17 this allows them to access £2.1bn of 'transformation' funding, not new money but part of the £10bn NHS funding agreed in the 2015 spending review. The main bulk of this £2.1bn will go to emergency care, and smaller pots for efficiencies and transformations in service delivery.

The first thing to say is that these are not 'local' in any meaningful way. Despite their 'localizing' objective these STPs are massive structures covering on average 1.2 million people, merging local authorities and CCGs. Its hard to see how bringing together an average of five CCGs into one group could possibly lead to more local control over planning and securing good deals with local providers. If the last three decades of neoliberal economics and the consolidation of finances into a smaller number of corporate hands is anything to go by, its hardly going to put commissioning power in the hands of civil society.

Secondly, the timescale for the creation of STPs makes it impossible for these local actors to even call a meeting let alone carry out a serious strategic and inclusive exercise for the next five years of services over such large population sizes. Despite not many people knowing anything about STPs, the final STP Delivery Plans were submitted on the 21st October. These full plans were not published, rather they were sent to NHS England for revisions, with a likely publication in mid-December. On the 23rd December 2016 CCGs have to sign two year operational contracts with providers, starting on 1 April 2017. Even for the most committed local health campaigner, even if you knew about these deadlines, the chances of actually reading the plans and then organising a genuine consultation about them are extremely unlikely. It also means that service user involvement and accessible services are principles that will not even get on the agenda, leaving STP members to carry out the Kafkaesque job of ticking the sixty diversity and inclusivity boxes that they are required to do knowing full well that the real stakeholders have been left without any meaningful role to play. At its very best, this offers local health groups the option of a headless chicken approach to health management. At its worst it will lead to a radical decline in patient care and safety.

Now for the really funny bit. The principle requirement for STPs is that the CCGs and providers that form the main bulk of these STPs have to square the circle of NHS funding by cutting expenditure enough to stay within their budgets for 2016–2017. If they over spend, and do not improve patient care at the same time they will not be able to get any further 'transformation' funding. But if the books already don't balance, are STPs are just being tasked to cull staff and services by the end of 2017 in order to secure future funding?

This cuts-dressed-as-innovation is a familiar slight of hand for those health warriors who were involved in the creation of CCGs where cuts in budgets combined with devolution of healthcare provision to local services and penalties for not implementing impossible targets worked very well in shifting the burden of responsibility from the government to local stakeholders. The task of balancing the NHS's books in one year while at the same time improving patient care is literally impossible leaving STPs with the option of failing or gaming. This is not just a sanitised process of ticking boxes, its actually about cutting services and, increasingly, getting people back to work. With the advent of the DWPs new Health and Work Programme in April 2017, this derogation of duties of care will get worse.

Although the failures of a target-oriented healthcare system are widely understood, with even Jeremy Hunt calling for more transparency and fewer targets, the reality is that the entire system of monitoring public services rests on measuring targets that clinicians did not set. Unless this top-down model is addressed, then the appeal for innovation in healthcare becomes just another ministerial dictate with more than the usual hint of irony.

The first proposal of this book is that at some point the people working in healthcare are going to have to reject the targets set for them in Whitehall. Yes, we are going to have to negotiate with senior management about what targets are set and by whom. On a policy level this means securing a real commitment to local autonomy in decision making that responds to local needs and resources. On the frontline this means organising ourselves for the battles ahead – and the possibilities that we have to continue to work under a structure that is diametrically opposed to good patient care.

Mindless measurements and nonsense data

The other key problem is that this system of targets is maintained by a rigid system of measuring performance and outcomes. Even putting aside the misinformation that gets circulated about NHS finances, there is no shortage of data in the NHS. The problem is what sense we can make of it.

This drive to measurement in the NHS started out with Blair's proposal that you cannot manage what you cannot measure. The problem is that just because you are measuring something does not mean you are actually managing it. Measurements only work if they inform better patient care, which, in the current climate, they do not, and in many cases are quite the opposite. We all know that much of the data that is collected makes no sense at all because it is designed around a model of care that is chopped up into neat pieces. What gets measured is not patient care, but carved-up part-care tasks such as waiting times and discharge rates. This Taylorist version of healthcare reduces the actual job that needs doing to part-processes – assessment here, medication there – rather than the actual job of responding to the whole human being in front of you. The measurements do not actually measure healthcare.

This system of measurement and reporting has a profound effect on how people are managed. Filling in forms becomes more important than finding the right treatment for a patient, and the clinician who wants to think about what is best for the patient is punished for inefficiency. It encourages clinicians to become mindless in their work, prioritising targets over the specific needs of the patient. Given that clinicians know this is happening, one way of coping with it is to stop thinking about it. To switch off our critical minds to the impact this has on patient care and safety.

For services in crisis these reductive measurements of care are used as a stick to beat the non-compliant clinician. A refusal to discharge a psychotic patient becomes a conversation about a backlog of online filing and a missing report from February 2014 with your line manager. This is not paranoid – it is what happens when people do not agree about delivering care and tired or inexperienced managers decide to enforce poorly designed project management techniques. It is a very common experience that these tools can easily become weapons in teams where there are conflicts over care. It is one explanation why mindless measurement tasks that cost millions in staff time and even more in staff disengagement are allowed to continue because nobody is prepared to speak up. This is a culture where nobody can afford to make mistakes and people manage workplace conflict by keeping their mouths shut.

This reliance on metrics as opposed to actual care is, I am going to suggest, the lived experience of a marketised health system. I am not technically saying that capitalism is to blame – I think the drive to neatify and deny complexity is inbuilt – but the attempt to fit ourselves into boxes, outputs and numbers is happening in a context of a particular economic model.

The second proposal of this book is that performance only matters if we are delivering the right things – and to do this we need to start measuring and collecting data on the things that matter to patient care and give up our addiction to mindless gaming.

Downgraded jobs and degraded workers

One of the things that is almost always overlooked in the NHS debates is the experience of the people delivering these services, which creates a substantial dehumanisation of the issues. According to the people working in it, the NHS runs on a 'pervasive culture of fear' – over one quarter of staff claim to be bullied and discriminated against, and when you add to this the startling fact that 30 percent of NHS staff are on benefits to supplement their low wages, the concept of precarity becomes real.

Precarious work is the new black in academic and policy circles with some good data coming out about low wages, temporary agency work and the impact of the 'gig economy' on the regulation of work. Precarious work is defined as work arrangements where workers are at risk of not being able to call on their basic employment rights and do not have the capacity to protect themselves from abuse at work. The growth of precarious work is linked to globalisation and the spread of a neo-liberal economic model, particularly the use of subcontracting chains and outsourcing as well as changes in work organisation such as 'flexible' working and lean production methods. These changes in workplace organisation are linked to work intensification and the use of lean working practices such as setting individual targets, standardisation of tasks and management practices such as 'command and control' management. This is not left-wing paranoia, it is a matter of employment relations fact.

Precarious work has been around for so long in the UK that the last time I used the term 'permanent work' in conversation, I was sprayed with coffee as the person I was talking to sputtered that it was preposterous for me to expect any guarantee of work. I had to explain the difference between having a permanent contract and a lifetime guarantee of work. This person was the UK director of the second largest private employment agency in the world, a rapidly growing 282 billion Euro a year industry, the legal and visible tip of the contract and agency labour iceberg. The delusion of safety of employment has truly been bred out of us, along with expectations of social and employment protections, pensions, training or career progression.

Those of us who still have jobs are supposed to feel like the lucky ones, but in these deregulated times, it might not feel that way. There are three rather obvious reasons why the people actually delivering healthcare in the UK are so overlooked.

First, the reality of working life is very low down on the political food chain in a system that is dominated by politically set targets and appeals to managerial efficiency. Employment relations have not been considered important in the health debate so far – degraded into a story from the 1970s of old male trade unionists trying to keep their gold pensions and work to rule. This lack of interest in working people is exemplified in the example that the NHS's own workforce database – the Health and Social Care Information Centre – did not collect information about its own internal labour agency, Bank, until

November 2014. The HSCIC still does not collect information on the number of external contract and agency workers providing NHS services or, more importantly, whether it makes a difference to patient care.

The second reason that so little is known about health workers is that the people delivering these services are just too scared to engage in the debate. When you work in a precarious job you are highly vulnerable to precarious states of mind, completely counterproductive for people employed to contain the anxieties of others. It is not just the migrant workers working as nurses for private employment agencies who feel insecure – it affects everyone working in this system. Precarity is inclusive, with even senior clinicians on permanent contracts unwilling to join the ranks of the self-employed by raising patient safety concerns with management.

This is a culture where nobody can afford to make mistakes and people manage workplace conflict by keeping their mouths shut. It means that people working in health and care are often disorientated by a sense of 'liquid fear' where a sense of fear permeates every aspect of our working and home lives. This is a state of mind where distinctions between serious and less serious workplace problems cannot be made. The smallest mistake becomes the end of your career, and you wake up bolt upright sweating at three in the morning wondering how you are going to handle the next informal chat with your line manager. This fear goes right up the management chain of NHS leadership, such as the previous head of NHS England, David Nicholson, reduced to talking about the very evident financial crisis only from the safety of retirement and a peerage.

A third reason why so little is known about employment relations is because of the nature of the work. Caring for people is not like working in IT. Emotional work has never been highly valued in our society, reflected in the bad pay and the ease with which emotional workers are blamed for systemic failure – easier to blame a nurse than succumb to the anxiety of realising that our health and social care systems are failing.

When people are scared at work it results in witch-hunts, whistleblowing and tribal warfare. A working culture where staff meetings become an exercise in the yes/no game of talking around issues and walking on eggshells. If you add to this the compulsive drive for a 24/7 health system, you do not have to be mad to work for the NHS, but it is extremely likely.

Now, what I am about to say is going to sound a bit paranoid, but I want to make a suggestion that the downgrading of clinical jobs going on throughout the NHS is massively convenient for private healthcare providers. Bluntly, if you downgrade the job so that you do not need to employ highly qualified professionals, the job can be filled by anyone who is prepared to do the work at the price. Experienced clinicians in their fifties and sixties who become demoralised will drift off into private practice and early retirement, leaving behind an increasingly outnumbered professional class to defend services. New generations of clinicians are not replaced; instead non-clinical staff are employed to cut the waiting times by holding patients before an actual clinician can see them. I will admit that I am of the paranoid persuasion, but if the experience of other sectors and three decades of public sector reform is anything to go by, this trend can safely be described as a corporate game changer. If I were an ambitious management consultant working for a major private employment agency (PrEA), I would note that there is nothing much to stop me taking over the future staffing of healthcare.

To even begin to address the downgrading of jobs two things need to happen – first, the way people are managed needs to shift from targets to teams and actual leadership developed on that basis; second, those of us working on the front line need to build our collective case for reform of the working conditions and contracts we are being forced into. We need to organise an upgrade. The attitudes and capacities of frontline managers and workers to address these workplace realities are probably the most important factors in building decent working conditions. The strategic aim of this book is to help healthcare workers understand the nature of the problems they are facing and their collective capacities in tackling them.

Actual leadership

As a society we have lazily allowed jobs in healthcare to become too hard, sometimes impossible, by playing games with health targets, provoking an often deeply cynical response by clinicians. This is a response to two things. First, the rate at which changes are taking place in our sectors makes it very hard for us to understand the climate we are working in. Second, despite the emphasis on relationships within healthcare there is very little evidence that we are able to find a way of working collaboratively within our teams.

One of the most devastating examples of what can happen as a consequence of workplace cultures is the Mid-Staffs case, researched in detail by the Francis inquiries. There is a direct link between working in a clinical environment where concerns cannot be raised and quality patient care. The ultimate problem with not addressing how staff are being treated is that the patient gets to carry the consequences when things go wrong.

Despite there being a whole research industry around team working and improving patient care – such as the Kings Fund – attempts to manage healthcare have largely focussed on senior management and policy. Because researchers and academics are not actually running the country, although the research exists – and in one-page brightly coloured digestible form so that they can be thrust at ministers in a lift – the productivity facts do not matter much on the frontline.

Frontline teams and managers operate in a parallel universe – often totally cut off from management decision making, training and informed research. Many frontline managers avoid the senior teams for fear of somebody noticing some fat in the system, ending in a feeding frenzy. People on the frontline are trying to constantly solve the jigsaw puzzle of insufficient funding, duty of care, patient safety, staff engagement and long-term planning only to find there are two jigsaw pieces missing – one called Actual Thought where information can be processed, discussed and responded to and the other called Actual Decision-Making Power at the level of the team. In effect, the missing elements of Actual Leadership.

The third proposal of this book is to adopt a model of leadership which is likely to decrease rather than compound precarity and build Actual Leadership at the level of frontline services. The model of managing teams that is proposed within this book draws on a tradition of what is sometimes called democratic leadership, where teams are the primary unit of management and hold the collective responsibility for performance. This model was developed in the manufacturing sector in the 1980s, using a Japanese model of team building – a 'support and stretch' as opposed to a 'command and control' culture which emphasises interdisciplinary and experiential learning and importantly is linked to high clinical results. Some of us have been in this movie before – back to the 1980s of team working and quality circles, autonomy in practice and flat hierarchies, just minus the shoulder pads and 'Frankie Says' T-shirts.

A crisis is not a catastrophe

One of the problems with framing our thinking about the future of jobs in healthcare within a broad definition of precarious work is that it has a catastrophising tendency. In a context of global recession, privatisation and flexibility, the problem of precarity is too big to take on. We are all doomed. This not only causes a catastrophisation of the problem of precarious work, but it serves to obscure concrete steps that can be taken to reduce labour insecurity.

Most healthcare workplaces are under enormous strain, and as a defence against this reality many clinicians work in silos. This can lead to workplace cultures much like a seventeenth-century French court – a preoccupation with the minutiae of court procedures and lace cuffs rather than the blood and guts of economic crisis and protecting decent services. The rise in mental health problems of health workers points us to the urgent need to find a more robust way to help healthcare workers survive work than sending them on mindfulness courses and nudging them to lose weight.

On some level, most of us are scared about the future, but it is important not to confuse an emotional reality of insecurity with structural insecurity of the employment relationship. We often mix up, for example, job stability, defined as length of job tenure, and job security, a much more complex and 'messy' idea involving perceptions, probabilities and anxieties. Our sense of job security is not just about the job – it is about what we think would happen if we lost it and involves external factors like changes in welfare and affordable housing.

This line between crisis and catastrophe is the important one to walk in defending decent jobs. The reality is that we have not all become precarious to the same degree at the same time. Some people working in healthcare are still in a position to protect their interests. Although the final outcome of the junior doctors' dispute has yet to be lived out, public support plus a clear platform for negotiation and sufficient internal pressure to kick the British Medical Association (BMA) into action has drawn one of the battle lines for decent jobs in healthcare. It is not that I am politically or socially aligned to most junior doctors that I support them – but because I know that if their working conditions go down, so will mine. Defining the battle lines where there is some collective capacity to defend jobs is key.

It is also a mistake to airbrush out collective action and the reality that when you work in healthcare you need to join a trade union. Precarious workers are organising all over the world because they need to rather than because they hold a unified ideological position, comrade. Dismissing trade unions is a strategic error, whatever your politics, because in healthcare we continue to have strong unions that, with all their faults and warts, when mobilised are the only show in town for improving working conditions and wages.

To be sure, trade unions were late to the game and continue at times to drag their heels doing the much needed job of organising precarious health workers. But this is part of the ordinary reality that we are all guilty of not seeing the extent of the changes ahead and that unions have declining resources as demand goes up. Sound familiar? To remove trade unions with a broad ideological sweep of the hand not only denies the work they do with precarious workers, but also misses important opportunities for much needed change at the level of the workplace.

Working in healthcare has always been a dual task of both improving and surviving healthcare systems. If the entire history of industrial relations is anything to go by this will only happen if teams can operate collectively and enlist the support of clinicians and managers throughout the structures they work within. Sorry, there is no way around this; in order to secure better working conditions we have to be organised.

This is the fourth proposal of the book – that we need to organise ourselves sufficiently to establish a negotiating platform for decent jobs. To not join a trade union as part of this strategy is just shooting ourselves in the foot. Whatever support does or does not exist in your networks, you still need to build solidarity relationships at work. Even if you cannot currently negotiate with management and your union branch has gone to sleep, it should not stop you from preparing for a future scenario where working conditions and wages are on the table. To do this requires finding ways to collectivise, formally or informally, in or outside of a trade union, but always without asking for permission.

A relational model of care

Individual attempts to secure decent work do not work, and even with supportive management, securing material changes always requires a powerful and organised drive. This presents us with a problem of how to build sufficiently strong relationships with the people we work with to act collectively.

Given the emotional nature of the work of care, you would think we would all be experts in forming relationships. But most working people cope with conflict and group dynamics by withdrawing into a 'bunker' – a safe place not disturbed by actual other people. Although many of us are naturally good at building intimacy, intimacy at work requires a framework to sustain it.

The fifth and final proposal of this book is that in order to survive in healthcare we have to build our relationships with each other – a relational model of care both for our patients and each other. Throughout this book are discussions about the principles and practices that underpin this model, taken from different educational, psychoanalytic and industrial relations traditions.

A relational model of care involves three things. The first is putting the job of work back in centre place as the main orientation for teams. The second requires those teams to agree some common principles that set the battle lines between what's fair and what's not both for the patient and the clinician. Because our principles in healthcare are compromised every day, these two elements can only be protected if we have genuine and functioning relationships with the people we work with. The third element of relationality is therefore to actively develop our relationships within the workplace – learning how to make friends and influence people.

One of the difficulties of getting on with people at work is that many of us working in healthcare have superegos like tanks – the internal voice that sees things in absolutes of right and wrong, black and white, you-must-do-this rather than what-is-realistic. It means that on an internal level, giving good care means challenging our internal judiciary and the part of us that wants to blame and shame others more than we want to understand them. Having humanising and genuine relationships with colleagues involves the internal work of showing a level of humanity to ourselves. Within this model, the capacity to deliver care rests entirely on having relationships at work that allow mistakes to be made, thought about and addressed without anyone being burned at the stake.

The proposal of this book is that surviving work involves focussing on our ability to see reality in all its ugly glory, allowing ourselves to get angry about it but still trying to understand it, learning to find help and relying on our relationships with others. To actually do this the proposal is to revive a tried and tested model of emancipatory education and psychodynamic ideas. Drawing on the work of two bearded blokes – the Brazilian liberation theologist Paulo Friere and the father of psychoanalysis Sigmund Freud – this book aims to provide a jargon-free, practical framework for building relationships at work.

This approach is good at building relationality because its central objective is of empowering the individual – what is sometimes called agency or self-efficacy – and increasing our capacity to take control over our lives. It is a model that respects the 'ordinary' expertise and authority of having experienced and survived work, recognising that we are capable of solving our own problems. This is a model of talking and listening and allowing other people to influence how we see the world. These practices are even more crucial in workplaces where management is not receptive to frontline workers making decisions about healthcare. It is precisely in the anti-relational workplaces that the methods of relationality are needed most.

Keep walking the line

Working in healthcare can be really depressing. I mean that in its existential rather than clinical sense. Many of us working in healthcare spend periods feeling hopeless – the belief that what we do matters eroded on a daily basis.

Many of us working in the public sector walk the thin line of surviving work and at times our relationship with work is abusive. As I wrestle with the emerging conclusion that my entire progressive-do-good life was a waste of time a deep weariness has set in. The messy slow work of building a life becomes devalued, and the daily work of being human is no match for this regime of self-righteousness, certainty and compulsory fitness. Embodied politics – you know, when you actually do what you say – becomes at best socially awkward and at worst career suicide.

Crisis brings us face to face with one of the unavoidable facts of life: that we are all dependent on each other. As the containment of public services breaks down, social anxiety goes up, and the temptation is to manage this by projecting our vulnerability into others. The demand for cuts is a defence against this anxiety precisely because it denies our inherent need for care. Even by drawing lines between people – between the sick and the fit, 'scroungers' and 'hard-working people' we can never successfully cut ourselves off from the reality that as human beings we are inherently vulnerable.

For people who have such concern for our patients we are showing pitiful little for ourselves and the people we work with. What follows in this book is my best shot at giving you some useful ideas about how to survive work in healthcare. If you do not have time to read this book I can summarise for you everything I know so far:

- Don't blame yourself: understand the social, political and economic factors that make your work what it is
- Don't keep calm and carry on: find a way to actually feel what you feel about that – from anger to the need to punch and spit, feel it and find ways to express it that will not end up with you losing your job
- Don't be brilliant: resist the temptation to be a superhero and single-handedly overcome the systemic failure of welfare capitalism; try to be an ordinary person
- Don't go it alone: just stop fighting the obvious that you have to get on with the people you work with enough to talk to each other and where possible collectivise around what is important at work

To draw and then hold the healthcare battle lines will require us putting down our ideological and clinical differences and freely associating with as many people as we can at work and across the UK's health systems. This is a psychological war we have entered into – and part of that battle is to associate with people across our sector, even those who are different from us, and hold to different ways of working. To listen to each other and be prepared to be influenced by what we hear. To support the individuals and groups that take up true leadership and to challenge those that maintain the political Noah's-arkism that dominates our professional and training bodies.

Ultimately, surviving work depends on how we treat each other. Whatever the outcomes of the continued NHS reforms, it matters if you ask people how they are and listen to the answer, support someone with a concern at the next supervision or join a union. It matters that you feel you belong at work and have enough connection with the people around you to ask for help or to offer it. Time to dig deep and become healthcare citizens, not just healthcare workers.

Reading

Armstrong D & Rustin M (2015) *Social Defences against Anxiety: Explorations in a Paradigm*. London: Karnac.

Brunning H & Perini M (Eds) (2010) *Psychoanalytic Perspectives on a Turbulent World*. London: Karnac.

Davis J & Tallis R (2013) (Eds) *NHS SOS: How the NHS Was Betrayed and How We Can Save It*. London: Oneworld Publications.

European College of Neuropsychopharmacology (2011) Size and Burden of Mental Disorders in Europe. *European Neuropsychopharmacology*.

Foresight Mental Capital and Wellbeing Project (2008) *Final Project Report*. London: The Government Office for Science.

Leys C (2015) Can Simon Stevens' Sustainability and Transformation Plans save the NHS? Centre for Health and the Public Interest. https://chpi.org.uk/wp/wp-content/uploads/2016/05/CHPI-STP-Analysis.pdf

Leys C & Player S (2011) *The Plot Against the NHS*. Pontypool: Merlin Press.

Main T (1989) *The Ailment and Other Psychoanalytic Essays*. (Eds) Jennifer Johns. London: Free Association Books.

Marmot M (2015) *The Health Gap: The Challenge of an Unequal World*. London: Bloomsbury.

Money-Kyrle RE (1951) *Psychoanalysis and Politics*. London: Duckworth.

Obholzer A & Zagier Rogers V (1994) *The Unconscious at Work: Individual and Organisational Stress in the Human Services*. London: Routledge.

OECD (2014) *Mental Health and Work: United Kingdom*. London: OECD.

Pollock A (2004) *NHS plc: The Privatization of our Health Care*. London: Verso.

Royal College of Psychiatrists, Mental Health Network, NHS Confederation & London School of Economics and Political Science (2009) *Mental Health and the Economic Downturn: National Priorities and NHS Solutions*. London: Royal College of Psychiatrists Occasional Paper OP70.

Taylor R (2013) *God Bless the NHS: The Truth behind the Current Crisis*. London: Faber & Faber.

The Health Foundation (2016) A perfect storm: an impossible climate for NHS providers' finances? http://www.health.org.uk/sites/default/files/APerfectStorm.pdf

Wilkinson R & Pickett K (2009) *The Spirit Level: Why More Equal Societies almost always Do Better*. London: Allen Lane.

2 Start where you are

"You can't change the data about discrimination in the NHS without understanding why it's happening."

Surviving work conversation: healthy organisations

PHILIP: The thing that makes organisations go wrong is that anxiety is feared, and instead of anxiety being moved up the system managers act to make the people below them anxious, and they then resist that anxiety. We see this in different ways – when politicians decide how clinicians should talk to patients, which is completely insane. The freedom that's absent from clinical work comes about from a fear of anxiety.

ANGELA: Targets and box ticking looks very logical and containing – but it's got absolutely nothing to do with the work. It's about containing the managers' anxieties.

PHILIP: Thinking only happens when people feel free to communicate with each other. Usually there would be an expectation that we as consultants, for example, are the experts. But one principle we have is that the work with groups is a partnership, and we have to assume when we're working with a group of people that they are expert in what they're doing. The mind of the human being is a story of consciousness – that the mind develops because we are driven by curiosity. We want to know, and we want to understand. But all of us will have explanations of our experience that don't develop – that are stuck – which frees you from the problem of thinking. Organisations, just like individuals, will create certainties which stop real thinking happening, which confines everyone to a particular way of being.

ANGELA: Talking about rigid thinking with healthcare workers takes us straight into a discussion about bullying, racism, power dynamics at work. This framework for understanding group functioning leads straight into being able to do organisational work.

PHILIP: Inquiry and not taking things at face value is important. For instance, a very common problem in any team is splitting. Usually the fixed belief that goes along with splitting is that the problem is to do with personality or 'personality conflicts'. The team has decided that the issues at work are down to individuals. These individuals become the problem and have to change. Actually individuals represent something that's going on deeper in the system and that they are being recruited to express something about the system.

ANGELA: When I'm doing mediation most of the work is about getting individuals separately to think about the other person involved and the organisation to put the problem in context. So that when they get together they have a different way of thinking about their position. When has it happened before? Is it unusual? All those sorts of questions.

To hear the full conversation with Angela Eden and Phillip Stokoe go to www.survivingworkinhealth.org.

Start where you are

A few weeks ago I did something I have been avoiding for about twenty years – I talked about racism at work. As part of the Surviving Work in Healthcare programme, I and a group of health and social care practitioners have been meeting and having conversations about the juicy topics of whistleblowing, bullying, fear and loathing in the NHS. The extracts at the beginning of each chapter in this book are taken from these conversations – and can be accessed on our website, www.survivingworkinhealth.org. The people involved are all friends and colleagues, people I admire and trust, but I was scared to say what I thought out loud.

Despite the blinding evidence, very few of us talk openly about the reality of institutional racism. The 2016 report from the Equality and Human Rights Commission – ironically published on the day that the UK A Level results came out – reminded us that we are far from a fair society when black and minority ethnic (BME) graduates earn 23% less than their white counterparts and will experience unemployment double the national average. The NHS is in no better shape. The NHS rests on what the Francis inquiries described as an 'endemic culture of bullying', one that has facilitated a growing crisis of structural discrimination and racism, staff burnout and stress, and with it a risk to patient safety.

At best we are working without a real understanding of our sector, at worst feeding a culture of Noah's-arkism – a split between different groups and individuals within our organisations – the people who still feel they have a place on the ark and those who do not. This is the phenomena where those people who still have decent jobs – or who are safely established on pensions or private practice, leadership positions in our professional and training bodies – are protecting what they have while turning a blind eye to those of us who are very-soon-to-be disestablished.

As a way of dealing with anxiety many of us fall into 'bunkers' or retreat into places where we can deny what is right in front of us. This includes racism, but it also includes the reality that any one of us can fall from grace within a system that denies systemic discrimination and the facts of working life.

At a societal level this can be understood as the growing split between the established and the disestablished – two very different realities but within the same settings. We see it every day in our services and with our patients – we now need to allow ourselves to see it in our professions.

Actual facts

The NHS has until now relied heavily on not collecting data on its black and minority ethnic staff, not publishing it and therefore not having to acknowledge the problem in the first place. But earlier this year the Workforce Race

Equality Standard was created to provide a way to measure staff equality in the NHS and encourage employers to ensure equal access to career opportunities.

In particular, recent research by Roger Kline into the racial makeup of the health service and the experience of BME staff has let the cat out of the bag. NHS leadership is described as the 'snowy white peaks' among a workforce that has seen its proportion of BME staff grow considerably in the last decade.

The research found the problem particularly bad in London, where 45% of NHS workers are from a BME background, compared to around 41% for the whole country. Despite much work to improve equality within the capital's health service, just 8% of London NHS Trust board members are from a BME background. Similarly, white staff in London are three times more likely to become senior managers than BME staff, and 25% of BME staff in the city consistently report they are discriminated against at work.

The NHS's workforce surveys also show that BME staff across England are more likely to be bullied at work and subject to disciplinary processes. The moment has come when we have to ask whether black working lives matter in the NHS.

If you are a patient, the answer is very much so. Research shows that the unfair treatment of BME staff is reflected in poor patient care. This is linked to our experience that a lack of diversity in teams reduces innovation and learning and that when staff do not represent their local communities they struggle to provide genuinely patient-centred care.

Standards and measurements of the scale of discrimination are extraordinarily important given the reality that nobody wants to talk about racism.

The policy context

The Health and Social Care Act (2012) introduced a profound change in the way healthcare was delivered and by whom.

In part to prove efficiency and in part to reflect political priorities there has been a growth in nationally set productivity targets to measure NHS performance. Although there is no problem with setting goals and monitoring, the problem in the NHS is that this has been done 'top down' so that ministerially set targets have become vastly more important than the traditional clinical outputs.

One of the problems is that targets are politically motivated, passed down from ministerial to management levels without due consideration of local needs and resources. Since the NHS was created there has always been a tension between supply and demand of healthcare.

One of the problems is that nobody really knows who is delivering services. The confusion and ignorance about who delivers care and how much they get paid is very much about the continuous privatisation and restructuring of the NHS and shift of commissioning powers to the local level, be that Primary Care Trusts (PCTs) or Clinical Commissioning Groups (CCGs). Over the last five years there has been a 50% increase in services provided by non-NHS providers, with expenditure rising from £6.6 billion to £10 billion. There are an estimated 53,000 private contracts in the NHS with 15,000 within 211 CCGs in community health services and secondary care. The primary problems of this privatised commissioning system relate to poor contract management and very low penalties for poor delivery. What we do know is that in 2014 half of the private mental health providers commissioned by NHS England to provide specialist care were not fully compliant with NHS standards.

The privatisation of the Commissioning Support Units in April 2016 set up to administer the NHS contracting process raises further concerns, principally by the Public Accounts Committee, about the governance and monitoring of those services provided by private providers.

You read that correctly.

The administrators in charge of managing third-party contracts will themselves be working for third parties.

At the time of writing this book the emergence of the almost completely unknown sustainability and transformation plans (STPs) has started to raise concerns about the future of health spending. In a deafening silence a total reorganisation and decentralisation of NHS decisions on spending over the next five years was announced in December 2015. Forty-four large geographical areas have been identified to set up 'local' groups made up of a very small number of senior healthcare providers and commissioners including representatives from clinical commissioning groups, local authorities, primary care and NHS Trusts.

STPs are charged to implement the NHS Five Year Forward strategy and to improve quality and develop new models of care; improve health and wellbeing; and improve efficiency of services. Their poisoned chalice is to square the circle of quality care by developing plans for integrating local services at the same time as managing major funding deficits. There is a tension in what is being asked of the STPs – contrary to the Health and Social Care Act, which aimed to increase competition in healthcare delivery, the STPs are asking NHS organisations and providers to collaborate. A key function for example will be to build care 'footprints' that create better collaboration between GPs, hospital specialists and social workers in providing social care.

Although the ambition to have locally determined and planned healthcare is important, what will be striking to people who work in healthcare is the likely failure of STPs charged with bringing about improved quality and interdisciplinary cooperation in healthcare. Even with an adequately funded healthcare system, integration and local management of services is the holy grail of good healthcare and sustainable services. Within a target-based, underfunded and privatised health and social care context it becomes impossible to imagine how this can be done.

It is also unclear how STPs can honestly look at quality of services in the current punative and regulatory context where healthcare providers are penalised for underperforming. This is inevitably going to lead to a lack of information and transparency in the STPs. Even on a basic level it is hard to imagine how already stretched STP members will find the time to meet and develop plans across such massive population groups, with the largest STP covering 2.8 million members.

This apparent 'decentralization' of decision making is reminiscent of the creation of CCGs where the increase in local decision making was met with a decrease in actual funding. There is a sleight of hand in these initiatives which gives 'choice' to local actors while at the same time limiting funds so severely that those choices are radically reduced. These changes have taken place so quietly that the burden of responsibility for delivering a national system of healthcare becomes devolved without due political process.

Despite genuine concerns about whether STPs can be set up in a way that enhances healthcare rather than shuts it down, this quiet revolution in planning and managing services has already taken place. STP functioning will be crucial in understanding the way that healthcare is commissioned and supplied in the future. STP capacity to propose major re-organisation of services – such as shutting or merging facilities – will inevitably have an effect on the jobs and conditions of the people working in them. Adding another level of small group management over large sections of services means that STPs are likely to be bad news for people working on the front line. To keep up to date with the development of STPs the *Health Services Journal* (HSJ) is doing a useful online map of the STPs as they develop (www.hsj.co.uk).

This privatisation of public services has been going on for a long time. Since the 1990s, liberal and coordinated market economies have experienced large scale reorientation towards global markets and flexible work structures. We have seen the massive growth of attempts to open up healthcare markets to private providers – most recently the highly contested Transatlantic Trade and Investment Partnership (TTIP) between the US and the EU, which aims to secure access to markets, including the NHS. The NHS has gone through three major periods of restructuring since the 1980s, involving the Public Finance Initiative (PFI), which opened the doors to private finance and the decentralisation of budgets to allow for local 'competition'.

This has inevitably led to the growth of multinational corporations (MNCs) and the extensive use of global supply chains. From pharmaceutical companies to private employment agencies (PrEAs), digital tech providers to Alternative Investment Funds (AIFs) or private equity, these global organisations are now major players in the delivery of healthcare. This is not a Marxist conspiracy, it is a global reality that as access to previously public services grows, the potential for MNC expansion does too. It is not a coincidence that Simon Stevens, the current chief executive of NHS England, previously worked for United Health Group, the American MNC which owns Optum, its health services wing. The strategic advantage of MNCs is that they are large and can manage long-term expansion into new markets like the NHS by subsidising services and securing large and long-term contracts. The risks to the NHS are significant – from the poor negotiation of contracts by civil servants to the insecurity of short-term investment strategies of private finance.

As austerity continues, these private contracts are likely to be downgraded to compete with ever stringent budgets. This will undoubtedly affect the employment contracts of the already flexible workers within these companies and private employment agencies. Within the next ten years the clinicians and managers in these private companies who came from the public sector will have retired or moved, leaving a new generation of workers without any living memory of good clinical practice or decent work. Given that there is little to no governance of private contractors in the NHS, this will happen without even the slightest fuss over patient safety.

Most people who work in healthcare consider themselves to be employed by the NHS. However a growing number are working for private contractors, are working for private employment agencies or have a dubious status of 'self-employed'. For example, according to the National Council of Voluntary Organisations (NCVO) an estimated 437,000 third-sector workers are employed in health and social care with 115,000 in residential care.

Much of the UK's care work is being carried out by third-sector organisations – much of the work is voluntary or provided by trainees, such as psychotherapists in the UK. We are also seeing the growth of religious organisations sub-contracted to provide public services, such as welfare services in Scotland and in Kent.

One of the inherent conflicts for third-sector organisations is how public funding influences the principles on which they were established. This is acutely the case for charities, who legally cannot take a political position on the economic and social policies that are increasing the demand for their work. It means that third-sector organisations have to walk a very thin line between continuing to access government funding and taking a position on the link between poverty and health.

The lack of core funding for charities means that their accounts, although not technically corrupt, are often squeezed to fit the reporting requirements of donors. It means that core salaries are hidden under 'project coordination' and numerically defined outputs exaggerated to satisfy demands for value for money. All the while the unsustainability of many services in a climate of economic crisis and austerity is denied.

People get sick in a recession

Another overlooked reality in healthcare is that demands for services go up in a recession, from mental health services to medically unexplained symptoms. You do not have to spend much time in an Accident and Emergency (A&E) ward to see the connection between an economic and a health crisis.

The Joseph Rowntree Foundation produces regular updates about poverty in the UK and chilling figures about the rise in child poverty since 2008. An estimated 21% of UK adults are living in poverty – which goes up to 29% of UK children if we include housing costs in the calculations. The costs of poverty to the taxpayer comes to £78 billion a year in public services, £29 billion of which was spent on health services for conditions linked to poverty.

This data excludes the many people living in the UK who are 'dis-established' either by choice or necessity, living outside the social systems set up to protect them. Some, like people with addictions or long-term mental health problems, have exhausted state support or are unable to follow the treatment available. From illegal immigrants to those working in the grey economy, outside of labour regulation and national insurance systems, many people are excluded from health and social care, unable to give a name and address to even register at a GP practice.

In the UK there are an estimated 1.64 million unemployed, down from the heights of over 2.4 million following the economic crash in 2008. Although it's true that there are more jobs – it is important to understand the nature of these jobs, which are at best 'flexible'. Over half of the jobs created since 2008 are under the category of 'self-employed' – a much contested and misunderstood category of worker. Far from the fantasy that everybody is a company director, it generally means that you have no contract of employment, social security or National Insurance payments. Think Deliveroo rather than Alan Sugar.

There are currently 8.84 million people from ages sixteen to sixty-four who were economically inactive in the UK – a much larger body of people who are not receiving unemployment benefits. Again, the figures are contested, but welfare reform, particularly housing support, and the creation of Universal Credit has clearly led to a real decline in people's access to benefits in the UK.

The Marmot review and his subsequent book, *The Health Gap*, gives us an important examination of health in the UK, making a clear research link between social inequality and health. The research highlights that our levels of health are determined by our access and quality of housing, education, money, social environment and social position. Our gender, ethnicity, race and disability status are major determinants of whether we get sick, physically or mentally.

As health inequalities become an everyday reality it gets harder to kick stuff under the public interest carpet. I admit that I am a sucker for catastrophising, but with five million people in the UK living on less than a living wage we have no reasons whatsoever to be cheerful.

The UK's health policy is increasingly directed towards getting people back into work or off welfare benefits to reduce the financial loss to the economy. This emphasis on the financial costs of mental health has led to an important policy link between 'wealth and wellbeing' and the focus of welfare reform on individual 'health' and 'fitness' for work. This link between work and mental health is exemplified in: the government's restructuring of the Department for Work and Pension (DWP)'s Work Programme into the Health and Work Programme; the proposal in 2015 to locate NHS mental health services in 350 job centres; and a 2016 initiative to introduce job coaches into GP surgeries in Islington. These initiatives have received public criticism from clinicians and mental health networks.

The government's flagship reform combining six welfare programmes into one under the Universal Credit system has totally failed. Unrealistic and random cuts conflated by the failure of Atos, the large private contractor, to deliver the DWP's review of incapacity benefit, leaving millions of people without money to live.

Disability benefits have been transformed into personal independence payments where 'clients' can 'choose' their care from a range of 'service' providers. But incapacity benefit reform is driven by budget cuts, with decentralisation of budgets masking the reality of 20% cuts under the banner of customer choice. The Health and Work Service is currently being delivered by US contractor Maximus, tasked to assess anyone likely to be off work longer than four weeks, is playing a perverse game of assessing the presence of 'fitness' while avoiding actual 'sickness' by not providing any solutions to the problem. The reform of disability benefits and assessments characterised in Ken Loach's film *I, Daniel Blake* should be a compulsory aspect of training for anyone working in healthcare.

As supply of healthcare goes down the demand goes up, a trend that is likely to continue as long as the economic crisis does.

Decline in professional bodies and unions

Despite the growing and massive power imbalance between employers and employees, precarious workers are organising everywhere in the world: from cleaners in London to contract miners in Colombia, when people are really backed into a corner they can and do organise. However, the collective institutions that previously protected healthcare workers are in clear and consistent decline. The causes of this are hotly debated – from complacent leadership to the impending further restrictions on freedom of association through the Trade Union Bill – but the evidence is clearly in favour of a reduced collective voice in the employment relationship.

Since 2008 we have seen a decline in national-level collective bargaining along with large-scale cuts in public sector jobs. This has contributed to a decline in public sector union membership, the stronghold of trade unionism globally, and has put a downward pressure on union power in relation to wages and job security.

This is particularly stark in the health service, which is a predominantly low wage sector, and one where the growing insecurity of workers has put two pressures on both Unison and Unite, the main trade unions for health workers, as well as the more professionally focussed unions, the British Medical Association (BMA), the Royal College of Nursing (RCN) and the Royal College of Midwives (RCM). First, insecure workers are harder to organise and mobilise. This is for practical reasons that people work in a more isolated and fragmented way – long gone are the staff and smoking rooms that used to act as the collective spaces for workers. Work intensification and shift patterns mean that most people do not have the time to go to union meetings – even if they do join. Low-wage workers struggle to pay union dues despite the very clear need for legal and workplace support from reps. The complexity and increase in grievances and disputes at work has led to a massive rise in case loads for trade unions – with many branches overwhelmed with fighting fires, causing burnout of key activists and a lack of strategic vision in many cases.

However, there are many examples of precarious workers organising in the UK – often created out of specific disputes or issues such as minimum wages and often created by experienced networks of activists. This is true globally and in most sectors – where people are pushed into action they find a way to self-organise. Most recently in the UK we have seen the development of the Independent Workers of Great Britain (IWGB), which recently coordinated and won strike action over pay for the Deliveroo workers and which came out of long-running attempts to organise contract cleaners, mainly Latin American workers, in the University of London, culminating years of organising attempts by the 'wobblies', or Independent Workers of the World. Attempts to organise 'janitors' and service workers have been heavily influenced by activists in the US and the years of 'organising' drives spearheaded by the Service Employees International Union (SEIU). In mental health we have seen the development of the Psychology and Counselling Union – a small network that came out of a number of anti-austerity networks and headed by Andrew Samuels, a previous head of one of the large professional bodies. Although these new 'unions' are small and have limited bargaining capacity, they are a response to the growing dissatisfaction of precarious workers with working conditions, government policy and the reluctance of established union leadership to engage. Many are very good at campaigning and raising media awareness but because of their size are relatively weak in negotiating material benefits.

Without getting into a long-running debate about left-wing splitting, my own position is that these new unions are here to stay and we will see more of them – and that they are highly important in filling the gap that established unions can leave open by not being responsive to the needs of precarious work-ers. Industrial disputes arise quickly and will do so increasingly, and out of this we will see more groups emerging. I have spent much of my working life working with self-organised unions – and it is true that strategic organising can be macho and prone to heroics. By their nature these structures are weakly funded and find it difficult to maintain their organisations after disputes have been won or lost. These are not an alternative to established trade unions and all their resources, including their capacity to collectively bargain. However, they are an important way to raise issues and provide a political network for workers who are massively overlooked by more traditional institutions. Essentially we need both. Personally I support any that are genuinely active in representing workers but like to limit my time spent in the presence of heroic men who want to give me a political education.

Whatever your political view of trade unions, the reality is that the key reason why wages are going down is that precarious workers generally do not join unions and are hard to mobilise around collective bargaining. There are over 200,000 active workplace representatives in the UK doing what they can to organise people into unions. Most of them do this without pay and for the right reasons. Whatever your politics, unions up until this point have been the only show in town in negotiating wages, and their inability to defend the wages of health and social care workers is not a political problem but a genuinely social one. Trade unions have always had to walk the line between changing the employment relations system and helping people stuck in the current one – and activists see the balance between these two functions differently. Sometimes this duality is described as the difference between organising workers and servicing members – a false choice in my view, as both are crucial for our collective survival.

Since this is my book I am just going to say that although trade unions can be really disappointing, frustrating and slow, just join one. Seriously, just do it before you read Chapter 8, which really pulls out the moral big guns about solidarity at work.

The decline of professional bodies – although traditionally more conservative and split between their various functions as representative and also regulators of professionals – has also had an important impact on working conditions. In social care, for example, the Social Care Association closed in 2012, and 2015 saw the closure of the College of Social Work set up after the case of Baby P. Both of these bodies provided the professional framework for their sectors, and both were closed due to pitifully small deficits in funding. If we had wanted to maintain these bodies we could have, easily. Our professional bodies are in crisis – torn between defending the sector and their organisation, which increasingly cannot happen at the same time.

The structural conflict within the professional bodies becomes clear if we look at mental health services. In 2016 I went to a mental health conference to join a group developing a Wellbeing Charter for people working in psychological therapies. I normally last ten minutes in such environments before the existentials hit, but I took this occupational risk to show solidarity to the people I work with in mental health.

This meant running the gauntlet of shiny young folk promoting cognitive behavioural therapy apps and online courses, wellbeing at work industry reps, private contractors delivering the Work Programme and welfare assessments and private employment agencies and clinical psychologists measuring the impact of self-guided resilience manuals. An MP on a podium talks, apparently unencumbered by actual facts about his own government's inability to sign off the Universal Credit and unaware that being on welfare does not mean you are not in work, as 30% of NHS workers can testify.

As the discussions start about how we are going to build support for a Wellbeing Charter I realise that, for some, this is primarily a question of learning how to present the 'business case' and learn the creative accounting required to match targets and outputs with actually helping people. As someone who has spent most of my working life as a trade unionist I would like to suggest that the entire experience of industrial relations is that whatever financial argument you present to protect psychological therapies, actually doing it will require genuine political will on both sides. To simply adopt a business school logic creates just a fiction about 'going forward'.

To make matters worse I am sitting next to a rep from an online cognitive behavioural therapy (CBT) provider who is talking about how the clinicians they employ value the flexibility of working on a zero-hour contract. It appears she has not connected the growth of flexible work with the growing number of people working in mental health services who do not want to get out of bed in the morning because of the culture of fear they are forced to work in. Online therapy, a modality that is increasingly being promoted and used to deliver short-term mental health services, offers a narcissistic model where neither the patient nor the clinician ever has to be in contact with another troublesome human being ever again.

In Julian Lousada and Andrew Cooper's important book *Borderline Welfare*, they argue that when we lose the institutions of welfare we lose the general conditions that are necessary for care to take place. What we are left with is lots of activity that is done by increasingly vulnerable individuals trying to bridge a massive governance deficit. By not maintaining the institutions of welfare, the state fails in its duty of care to create the conditions under which health and social care work can responsibly be done.

Why consciousness raising helps you survive work

It is seriously tempting to look at all of this as just stuff you would rather not know. Not much you can do about it, right? Actually – and here is where my psychosocial biases come out – the first stage of building our capacities at work is to understand the realities of work. Whether you call it consciousness raising or just being informed, the first stage to tackling workplace problems is to understand your working environment.

In the educator Paulo Freire's writing he describes two stages of learning: a growing awareness of reality and a commitment to transform that reality. Within this model, learning involves consciousness raising where we learn about reality, including issues of power and oppression, through our own experiences and those of the people around us.

In learning theory, part of this process of seeing reality as it is involves tackling core assumptions, or threshold concepts that provide a basis or a perspective to the subject area and are transformative in that they trigger a change in consciousness, described by the psychoanalyst Bion as a transformation into 'being that something'.

Consciousness raising happens when we actually talk to people, particularly when we do this in small groups or one to one. At the risk of pointing out the painfully obvious to people who provide emotional labour, we learn stuff from talking to other people. It is important to have relationships where we can ask questions like, 'Am I being paranoid here, or are our targets this week just constructive dismissal?' Talking to other people is the only way of collectively understanding the external environment in which we work and the often complex dynamics that underpin them.

If we go back to the beginning of this chapter, which raised the painful issue of racism at work, we discover that even when we have the data we still have the enormous difficulty of tackling racism in our workplaces. The data does not express the deep and difficult emotions that are part of the experience of discrimination. Working with people who are not exactly like us and who are in pain and distress means that being offended by others is an occupational hazard. The issue is not whether we will be offended, rather what we do with the offence. If we nurture it and leave it unchallenged, it can turn to a hatred and a righteousness, producing a workplace where some people are seen as inherently better than others.

If we can start where we actually are, rather than where we would like to be, we stand a chance of talking honestly with each other about the future of our profession. It is also an important part of surviving work to have some sense that the systemic and political failures of our health system are not actually your fault. The only way to stop blaming yourself is to be able to accurately pinpoint how we came to be here rather than where we would like to be.

Reading

Bamber G, Lansbury RD, Wailes N & Wright CF (Eds) (2016) *International and Comparative Employment Relations: National Regulation, Global Changes*. Sixth Edition. London: Sage.

Bell D (1999) Introduction: Psychoanalysis, a body of knowledge of mind and human culture. In: Bell D (ed) *Psychoanalysis and Culture: A Kleinian Perspective*. London: Gerald Duckworth & Co. Ltd, 1–26.

Bennett D (Ed) (2012) *Loaded Subjects: Psychoanalysis, Money and the Global Financial Crisis.* London: Lawrence & Whishart.

Centre for Health in the Public Interest (2015) *The Contracting NHS – Can the NHS Handle the Outsourcing of Clinical Services?* Centre for Health in the Public Interest. Available at: https://chpi.org.uk/wp-content/uploads/2015/04/CHPI-ContractingNHS-Mar-final.pdf. Accessed 10 May 2016.

Cooper A & Lousada J (2005) *Borderline Welfare: Feeling and Fear of Feeling in Modern Welfare.* London: Karnac.

Croucher R & Cotton E (2011) *Global Unions Global Business: Global Union Federations and International Business.* London: Libri.

Davison S & Harris K (Eds) (2015) *The Neo-Liberal Crisis.* London: Lawrence & Whishart.

Dicken P (2016) *Global Shift: Mapping the Changing Contours of the World Economy.* London: Sage.

Dunleavy P & Carrera L (2013) *Growing the Productivity of Government Services.* Cheltenham: Edward Elgar.

Fleming P (2014) *Resisting Work: The Corporatization of Life and Its Discontents.* Philadelphia: Temple University Press.

Frege C & Kelly J (Eds) (2013) *Comparative Employment Relations in the Global Economy.* London: Routledge.

Gumbrell-McCormick R & Hyman R (2013) *Trade Unions in Western Europe: Hard Times Hard Choices.* Oxford: Oxford University Press.

Hall P & Soskice D (Eds) (2001) *Varieties of Capitalism: The Institutional Foundations of Comparative Advantage.* Oxford: Oxford University Press.

Lister J (2013) *Health Policy Reform: Global Health versus Private Profit.* Faringdon: Libri Publishing.

Resolution Foundation (2013) *Does It Pay to Care? Under-Payment of the National Minimum Wage in the Social Care Sector.* London: Resolution Foundation.

Resolution Foundation (2014) *Low Pay Britain 2014.* London: Resolution Foundation.

West M & Dawson J (2012) *Employee Engagement & NHS Performance.* London: Kings Fund.

West M & Dawson JF (2011) *NHS Staff Management and Health Service Quality.* Department of Health.

3 Precarious work

"A lot of people choose precarious work because they can get out of bullying in full time work. The problem is if they become sick or old."

Surviving work conversation: precarious work

ROGER: There are significant numbers of people in the NHS who have chosen to be in more precarious jobs because they may be able to earn more in the short term. And it gives them a degree of choice if they're people who feel actually I'm being bullied here – if I'm an agency worker I'm paid more per hour, but the problem is if they become ill or they become old they are seriously worse off. The reasons why organisations are prepared to pay more for agency workers is that they don't carry the long-term risks if staff become sick or retire with a pension.

ELIZABETH: You see that a lot in mental health services with people being unable or unwilling to navigate the NHS systems and going into private practice – some of them doing OK, others less so, but we don't know how many private practitioners or social enterprises are actually making any money. It's not just about money – it's also about things like skills degradation. If you work for a private employment agency there's a very low chance of getting training so in healthcare you have about five years before your skills can become quite defunct.

ROGER: That's going to be an issue around revalidation process. Agency nurses are not going to be doing more than the minimal upgrading because their agency on the whole isn't going to be paying for them to do anything more than the minimum. There is an issue, which I'm not sure has been thought through enough, about whether agency staff are going to be disproportionately disadvantaged, many of whom will be from black and minority ethnic backgrounds.

ELIZABETH: It's really interesting the lack of data on this. Coming from the mining sector, where contract and agency labour is the key health and safety issue, seeing the lack of regulation in mental health for example is terrifying. The research says one of the key risks around using contract and agency labour is around the casual workplace relationships that are no longer formed. There are critical incidents around the handover of shifts – people tend to not talk to the agency nurse in the same way they'd talk to a long-standing colleague. This patient has this problem, this piece of equipment is playing up – much less knowledge gets transferred, which presumably is going to have an impact on patient care. It's only very recently that the NHS has kept data on Bank staff – the internal labour agency in the NHS – so we don't really know what's happening as a consequence of precarious work.

ROGER: One of the consequences of the NHS announcing they are going to put a cap on agency staff numbers is that I suspect they will have to start to collect more data. One of the things you might want to map then is rates of agency staff against for example critical incidents.

ELIZABETH: I thought it was amazing that recently we had Simon Stevens waging war on private employment agencies, and we even had Jeremy Hunt saying they were costing too much money. What's terrifying is that we really don't know how much this is costing the NHS because no-one has collected this information.

ROGER: What's worse is that people like the Kings Fund are sceptical that the NHS can even do it. They are determined to drive the costs down, but there aren't enough staff permanently employed. The NHS has failed to make the work sufficiently attractive so that for some people it makes sense to go to an agency or to leave the profession. Simply saying we're going to cut out precarious working might hit the buffers when a chief executive says we're way over the four hours in A&E, get more staff in.

To hear the full conversation with Roger Kline and Elizabeth Cotton go to www.survivingworkinhealth.org.

The growth of precarious work

The battle lines for the NHS were re-drawn in 2015 when Simon Stevens, the head of NHS England, declared war on private employment agencies. In an attempt to get more nurses onto hospital wards and reach nationally set targets the NHS spent £1.8 billion on agency labour – double what was budgeted. In these flexible neo-liberal times, it is a rare thing to see an employer in favour of permanent contracts, particularly a public sector employer under pressure to make radical staff costs.

The debate around agency staff has exposed the smoke and mirror economics around precarious work in the NHS and has started to unpack the real costs to the taxpayer. The costs are hard to understand, distorted by penalties for missing targets raising the costs of trusts not having enough staff on shift and encouraging a retreat into short-term contracts and immediate staffing through agencies. For example, if we look at doctors each NHS Trust spends on average £5.8 million on employing locum doctors, £1.4 million of which goes to fees for the agencies. It means that when it comes to doctors the NHS pays twenty-five times the amount on agency labour as opposed to the money it spends on recruiting permanent staff. The costs of using precarious contracts just do not seem to add up.

The debate around precarious work is a defining one in the field of employ-ment relations, challenging established management practices and questioning the entire contents of business school libraries. Despite the trend of increasing flexibility and development of global production systems being in evidence since the 1970s, the precarious work debate is still active partly because of the complexity and range of precarious work forms that now exist.

Over the last thirty years we have seen a shift in the types and conditions of work in the UK – sold as an attempt to build flexibility into labour markets. Competitiveness became adaptation, facilitated by policies of privatisation and deregulation, particularly the removal of labour protections. The simple stuff of cutting the costs to employers to hire and fire – from cutting social costs by everyone becoming self-employed to cutting redundancy costs by putting everyone on fixed-term contracts – is not sophisticated.

Precarious work comes in many forms, including on call/daily hire, home-working, 'self-employed', freelance, temporary agency work (TAW), proba-tionary periods, student traineeships, apprenticeships, fixed-term temporary contracts and the infamous zero hours contracts. Young people are particularly affected by the growth of unwaged work or internships, widely regarded now as essential for securing paid work in the climate of a recession.

Precarious work raises a major regulatory problem to governments and public sector employers because of the 'externalisation' that is taking place. Externalisa-tion is the trend of obtaining labour from outside an organisation's boundaries, linked to the strategy of outsourcing and contracting out. With this externalisation of work comes an externalisation of the employment relationship away from a binary employer/employee relationship to include third parties, notably contractors, suppliers and private employment agencies (PrEAs). With this shift in the nature of the employment relationship come other externalisations – projections of risk and duties away from the principal employer, such as clinical insurance and continuing professional development. Additionally precarious workers themselves are vulnerable to problems of low wages, degrading of skills and all those unsavoury consequences of having no power in the face of an employer to secure basic pay and conditions. Unsurprisingly, then, there has been a continual fragmentation and decline in collective bargaining particularly around wages – mainly due to the lack of precarious workers who feel secure enough to join and become active in trade unions.

This process of externalisation is seen graphically in the growth of private employment agencies providing temporary agency work mainly to other huge companies. The employment agency industry reached Euro 282 billion turnover in 2015, with Adecco, Randstad and Manpower representing some of the largest multinational companies in the world. Over 30% of the global agency industry is controlled by just ten multinational companies. Clearly, they are not going anywhere.

This precarity was clear in 2008 when temporary agency workers were the first to lose their jobs. Over 50% of the jobs created in the UK since then are under the category of 'self-employed', a pseudo category of precarious worker where social responsibility and risk falls onto the individual. The delusion of safety of employment has truly been bred out of us as the 'gig economy' grows, taking with it our expectations of social and employment protections, pensions, training and career progression.

In the NHS there is an additional pressure on systems which has increased the use of contract and agency labour, namely the introduction of a target-based system. Since its creation, the NHS has struggled with the inherent conflict between funding and satisfying the needs of an ageing population. To address this the NHS has undergone a continual series of restructurings, intensified in the 1980s by the demand for the introduction of quasi-market systems and decentralisation of budgets including the creation of hospital trusts. The introduction of the Public Finance Initiative (PFI) opened the gates to private finance – ostensibly to reduce the cost to taxpayers – but also established the privatisation of the NHS, a project reinforced through the 2012 Health and Social Care Act. Although the financial gains of this strategy are highly contested these reforms have been maintained by successive governments, whatever their political colour.

The over-use of targets and penalties has directly led to work intensification in healthcare – and along with it a rise in 'command and control' management via New Public Management (NPM) practices, introduced as part of the UK government's economic policy to increase 'productivity' in public services and reduce social spending. This criticism of management in the NHS is not personal, it's clinical, if we take seriously the Francis reports on the existence of a 'pervasive culture of fear' and the impact on patient care.

For healthcare the growth of precarious work is a total disaster. Providing good healthcare is dependent on its staff. You cannot care for people without carers, despite the temptation to solve every health problem with an app. It means that employee engagement, or the degree to which people are motivated by their work, is the central focus of healthcare management. Employee engagement is a well-researched area of human resource management, identifying the need for mental and emotional stimulation, autonomy in decision making, career growth, skills development and, most importantly, social capital. This last one of social capital – or having relationships with the people you work with – is a key problem for precarious workers who tend to have relational insecurity because they are often excluded from teams and the collective activities that make up these relationships. This is practical, that the precarious worker is likely to have less contact with colleagues and be less able to attend the meetings and events where teams are actually built. Although many agency workers work long term in some units, most do not have as much space to form relationships at work.

The consequences of precarious work

I don't wish to blind you with industrial relations science, but precarious work is, well, precarious. It involves a rise in workplace insecurities such as continuity of income, skills development, progression and representation such that it 'places people at risk of continuing poverty and injustice resulting from an imbalance of power in the employer-worker relationship' (Trade Union Congress [TUC]).

First there is the issue of earning enough to live on. Britain is a low pay economy, with an estimated 20% of UK workers earning less than the living wage concentrated outside of the South East and affecting sectors such as sales, customer services and manual work the most. The average female private sector wage is £14,000, below the estimated minimum income for a single person. Because they are not paid enough to live on, 30% of people working in the NHS receive in work benefits – 30%!

Since 2009 the number of people earning less than a living wage has increased from 3.4 million to 5 million in 2014. The government's proposal in 2015 to cut £5 billion tax credits exposed the sheer scale of in-work poverty in the UK and also the strength of feeling of 'hard-working people' about regressive austerity cuts and where that left them. Despite no official government data, it is estimated that 1.5 million working people need housing benefit to pay their rent, a number that is going up by an estimated 10,000 people every month, exposing the real housing crisis for public sector workers. On top of this came the 'bedroom tax', which asked people to pay a levy for council and housing association tenants for any unused bedrooms in their home – a tax the UN reprimanded the UK government for as a human rights abuse. No wonder there was a staff shortage at Addenbrooke's given that a nurse's wage could not possibly cover the rent in Cambridgeshire.

The people receiving in-work benefits are mainly women and single parents, many of them working in health and social care. With pay freezes and a reduction in collective bargaining the real value of NHS wages has gone down over the past five years. Of the 1.4 million people working in social care, 160,000 are earning less than the living wage, particularly domiciliary carers who are paid only for their fifteen minutes of contact time and not their travel between clients.

The changes are stark in the public sector where jobs, although mainly low paid, were considered secure and compensated by having pensions and additional protections at work from the public duty of care to its staff. Since 2008, sickness absence has gone down. This is not just because everyone has officially become fit – the public sector still has one of the highest levels of absence (9.6 days on average) compared to other sectors (7.7 days) – but because with public sector cuts come a climate of fear, where more people keep working until something goes very wrong. For healthcare workers this is a real paradox, the very opposite of good health policy that emphasises early intervention rather than working until you drop.

Second, when people are precarious they are vulnerable to exploitation and discrimination.

The lack of legal protections for precarious workers and regulatory power to monitor employers has inevitably led to a shameful rise in discrimination at work in the UK. Despite higher educational attainment, black, Asian and ethnic minority (BAME) workers are twice as likely to be in insecure forms of employment such as temporary contract or working for an agency, and BAME workers with degrees are two and a half times more likely to be unemployed than white workers with degrees. Black workers with degrees are paid 23.1% less on average than white workers with degrees. And that is just the data, not touching on the lived experience of precarity at work for BAME workers.

Third, precarious workers are less able to keep and develop their skills and therefore are less likely to progress in their professions.

Unsurprisingly, health workers need not just to have skills but must also maintain them. This is not just a question of maintaining technical competence – continuing professional development (CPD) is an important aspect of maintaining a sense of competency and self-confidence for practitioners whose abilities are challenged by a system that over-emphasises targets over clinical care. Most professional codes are very specific about the training requirements for professional registration, but the funding of this system has changed over time. Core training is increasingly paid for by the individual, with the costs of initial clinical training high because of the length of time and placements that they require.

For the largest group of health workers – nurses – the future of training is not looking good. Despite a sustained campaign to protect training bursaries from 1 August 2017, all new nursing, midwifery and allied health professional students will have to secure student loans to get training. Training to be a nurse costs the individual, no longer the state. At the same time this decision was made the future of Health Education England (HEE), the training body for healthcare professionals, swung in the balance over a proposed 40% cut in their funding and staff. Workplace training has been in decline in the UK for the last two decades – an easy cost to cut in the short term. However, the long-term costs of not investing in the next generation of clinicians result in important consequences, not least the trend to increase non-clinical and low-wage jobs in the NHS, managed by a decreasing number of overstretched and experienced clinicians.

It means that the real cost to patient care of using precarious workers is actually not known.

Downgrading clinical jobs

The trends in precarity are clear if we take mental health services, always regarded as the poor cousin; in 2015 the public health bodies NHS England and Monitor proposed that mental health services should face an additional 20% cut in funding despite the rise in demand for services. Partly because of the stigma attached to mental health problems and the confidentiality inherent in the work, not much is known about the mental health workers delivering these services. During 2016, in response to this lack of data, I carried out the Surviving Work Survey of the working conditions of mental health workers. To see the full results of the survey and a national map of working conditions go to www.survivingworksurvey.org. What follows is a summary of some of the trends we are seeing.

Although campaigning for mental health awareness and increased funding of services is evident, the current economic argument for mental health services is based on the unacceptable working conditions of thousands of mental health workers. From psychological wellbeing practitioners (PWP), to Increased Access to Psychological Therapies (IAPT) workers in job centres, to the clinicians employed by Maximus and Atos to carry out welfare assessments, working in mental healthcare settings might be posing significant health risks to both clients and clinicians.

The confusion and ignorance about the employment relations system in mental health are very much about the continuous privatisation and restructuring of the NHS and the 2013 shift of commissioning powers to the local level.

However, this also exposes a range of employment relations problems faced by mental health workers, including the growth of self-employed workers, short-term contracts for private contractors, agency labour, the use of unwaged labour or honoraries, the insecurity of 'permanent' staff in the NHS and the retreat into private practice. We will look at each problem in turn.

The advent of agencies is nothing new in healthcare, but with the massive rise in demand for mental health services, NHS cuts and waiting lists of between six and eighteen months we are now seeing the creation and expansion of private contractors and employment agencies for mental health workers. Because of the intense insecurity of agency work and the fear of blacklisting of individual self-employed therapists, nobody wants to talk about this growth of third parties in mental health, and, as a result, not much is known about them.

The growth of precarious work is part of a national campaign to downgrade mental health services. Under the NHS's IAPT the main bulk of services are low-intensity 'wellbeing' programmes, based on a diluted model of cognitive behavioural therapy (CBT). These interventions only look at the thought patterns and behaviours of the individual and do not look at external realities or underlying causes for mental health problems. The model, in its very diluted sense only looks to quickly change the way people think and respond to problems, at best a first aid approach to mental illness.

For low-intensity CBT patients can expect four to six sessions, and even high-intensity services are generally capped at twelve sessions. Most patients experiencing depression or anxiety will be given six sessions only. You do not need to be a psychoanalyst to wonder if recovery in six weeks is in any way realistic. This service is delivered by psychological wellbeing practitioners (PWPs), a formalised and standardised role with intense targets of eight to ten satisfied clients a day.

Under IAPT the main bulk of services are low-intensity 'wellbeing' programmes delivered by PWPs. The work of PWPs is formalised and standardised to the extent that if a patient does not pick up the phone for an initial assessment within the allotted fifteen-minute time period they are referred back to their GP, presumably to wait for a further six months. Within these services it is all too easy to develop a hatred for the patient who keeps clinicians on the phone for too long, making it impossible for them to meet their recovery quota. Under these conditions the only way to responsibly help patients is to refer them on to other more intensive services. This situation exposes therapists to potentially precarious states of mind, from increased anxiety to vulnerability to bullying, a systemic problem within the NHS where the precarity for mental health workers is completely counterproductive for people employed to contain the anxieties of others.

We also know that the big PrEAs including Reed and Manpower, yet to specialise in clinical services, are providing labour for the call centres and online services that patients are fed through in order to access NHS services. It means that the people acting as the first point of contact for patients trying to access mental health services are unlikely to have any clinical training or to be able to offer the clinical support needed by people in distress and crisis. In IAPT for example a patient's mental health conditions are assessed over the phone during a twenty-minute call carried out by a PWP, someone who does not need to have clinical training to do this. Although the reality is that most PWPs will have at least an undergraduate qualification in psychology, this in no way prepares them for the nature of contacting people who have been on long waiting lists and who may well have complex problems. As a result some IAPT services find it difficult to employ PWPs because the pay and support for the role is dangerously inadequate. This raises questions about the duty of care of agencies dealing with vulnerable people, which is a growing reality given the length of NHS waiting lists and the inevitable rise in patient distress this creates.

Although currently most of the people working as PWPs are clinically qualified, principally as counsellors, their job is not to provide a space where patients can actually say what is on their mind. The work is scripted, manualised and always leads to one compulsory outcome, which is that everyone feels well. PWPs who offer more support, mainly through giving more time and going off script, are forced to keep this secret from employers because it breaks their contract of employment, leaving them to carry the full ethical and clinical consequences of their interventions.

This model of 'wellbeing', to be clear, can under no description be considered as therapy. Four to six sessions of mechanised interventions and questionnaires in no sense counts as therapy – cognitive or behavioural. There is also a complete denial of the reality of mental illness and the complexity of treating people with more than one issue (read: most people), which literally cannot be done using such short-term interventions. It is actually insane.

Clinicians know this but often cannot say it because they fear they will lose their jobs. Many clinicians, particularly the more senior high-intensity therapists, have raised their concerns but are met with complete impotence by managers tasked with reaching recovery targets within a rigid system of short-term work.

As if the system could get any more dehumanised, to add insult to injury, tucked away in the 2015 budget was the proposal that IAPT services should be introduced to 350 job centres in the UK – the 'psychologization' of poverty where unemployed people are forced by precarious PWPs to internalise a global economic and social crisis. In this scenario it's hard to imagine who needs the most help, the client or the clinician.

A growing percentage of IAPT services are provided by private and third-sector contractors and labour agencies who are literally buying up the growing NHS waiting lists. At the time of writing this book, there appears to be a particular growth in precarious work to provide IAPT services in Child and Adolescent Mental Health Services (CAMHS) as the Child and Young Persons (CYP-IAPT) services starts to be rolled out in England.

As with all externalised employment relations, it is not just the contract of employment that gets passed over to third parties, it is also the responsibilities of employers. Many people working in the NHS via agencies receive no training or supervision, raising questions about the duty of care to clients and employees. My research carried out in 2016 as part of a national survey of working conditions of mental health workers (Surviving Work Survey) suggests that 80% of private contractors and agencies do not provide clinical insurance, raising questions about professional liability.

A growing number of people working in mental health, particularly therapists and clinical psychologists, are registered as sole traders or self-employed. This raises important questions not just about professional liability but also clear lines of duty of care. Many mental health workers when asked who they work for will say the NHS – but the reality is that they may be self-employed, which puts a profound confusion into the question of clinical and employers' responsibilities.

The second employment relations problem in mental health services relates to internships, or the widespread use of honorary and unwaged therapists. The most important part of your training as a counsellor or psychotherapist, along with your own personal therapy, is to carry out clinical work. In order to train as an adult psychodynamic psychotherapist, for example, and become an accredited member of a professional body you have to work part-time – usually one to three days a week for between four to eight years as a psychotherapist. The problem is that the trainee is not paid. There is currently no comprehensive data on how many psychotherapists work unwaged as honoraries, but with approximately 6,000 psychotherapists being trained every year a conservative estimate is that 2,000 full-time psychotherapy jobs are covered by unwaged workers. This number goes up massively if we include counsellors and psychological therapists. It means that a substantial percentage of the psychotherapists working for the NHS, the big third-sector providers such as Mind and many local mental health charities, are not actually being paid.

The professional bodies that require clinical hours for training and professional registration are complicit in this system of unwaged work leading to the curious situation that the bodies charged with building a sustainable profession are currently not able to do that. If there is a political cause worth fighting for it is to make the demand for our professional bodies to organise a platform to negotiate wages.

As a result this is a profession open primarily to people from families rich enough to support them. There are some who work full time and do the training on top, but there is a real risk (as in other fields such as the media and the arts) that the great majority of practicing therapists will be people from affluent backgrounds. That is not to say that rich people make worse therapists than poor people, but it does raise important questions about class and power both clinically and within the profession.

The third employment relations problem relates to mental health workers employed by the NHS. In most cases the days of 'permanent' contracts are over, with cuts in funding and increasingly short funding cycles meaning many of the jobs are fixed and short term. Most NHS services are understaffed, particularly in CAMHS and Community Mental Health (CMH), leading to an emerging gold rush for private contractors and agencies. It means that a growing number of mental health workers although providing services to the NHS work as self-employed contractors and often through third sectors or charities providing contracts.

Just because an NHS provider is a mental health charity and provides much needed low-cost treatment in no way means it is a good employer. In our survey there was no difference in workplace problems between private providers such as the Priory, charities such as Mind and working in mental health trusts. The conflict among budgets, recovery targets and the demands of decent work is irreconcilable pretty much everywhere under the current system.

The insecurity of NHS workers has profound implications for 'workplace fear' and creating cultures where clinicians are reluctant to raise concerns about patient care. Despite the important debate going on now about raising concerns in the NHS, the reality is that precarious workers are unlikely to speak up for fear of victimisation and job loss.

As a result, many experienced psychotherapists have retreated to private practice, unable and unwilling to navigate a broken system. Many make enough money to survive in private practice but only after having spent most of their working lives in the NHS, leaving their pensions intact. This generation of psychotherapists will retire within the next five to ten years, leaving behind a whole generation of self-employed psychotherapists, many of them working within social enterprises and charities, who will never earn enough to cover the basics of pensions or sick pay. It is not to say that private practice does not offer massively needed services – it does, and a careful assessment and referral can make the difference between life and death. But it increasingly means that services are accessed only by those who can afford it.

It is a growing possibility that we are within a decade of the therapeutic professions dying out. As we become de-professionalised, downgraded and demoralised and our experienced leadership retired or retreated into private practice, this leaves the gates open to private providers to fill the gap, and very quickly. This leads us forward towards a mental health service made up of tick boxes and compulsory wellness – a ruthless regime of can-do contractors and labour agencies.

As long as mental health workers are working quietly and diligently under precarious conditions without any attempts to collectivise the NHS will never respect the people who work for it. In a context of deteriorating mental health services, the fact that mental health workers are an unorganised and silenced group of public servants is a matter for both professional and personal ethical concern.

It means that there is a pressing obligation within our professions to allow ourselves and encourage each other to look at the trends in precarious work so that we can prepare a coordinated response. As long as we are still denying this reality or pretending we still have a place on the ark, we will not address the systemic issues. Although knowing this reality will evoke fear and loathing in us the plus side is that it might make us angry enough not to waste a good crisis.

Reading

Armstrong D and Rustin M (2014) *Social Defences against Anxiety: Explorations in a Paradigm*. London: Karnac.

Bauman Z, Bauman I, Kociatkiewicz J & Kostera M (2015) *Management in a Liquid Modern World*. Cambridge: Polity Press.

Bentein K & Guerrero S (2008) The employment relationship: Current research avenues. *RI/IR* 63(3):409–424.

Carter B, Danford A, Howcroft D, Richardson H, Smith A & Taylor P (2013) 'Stressed out of my box': Employee experience of lean working and occupational ill-health in clerical work in the UK public sector. *Work Employment Society* 27(5):747–767.

Dicken P (2016) *Global Shift: Mapping the Changing Contours of the World Economy*. London: Sage.

Doogan K (2009) *New Capitalism? The Transformation of Work*. Cambridge: Polity Press.

Francis R (2010) *Independent Inquiry into Care Provided by Mid Staffordshire NHS Foundation Trust January 2005 – March 2009*. Vol. 1. London: The Stationery Office.

Francis R (2013) *The Mid Staffordshire NHS Foundation Trust Public Inquiry Report of the Mid Staffordshire NHS Foundation Trust Public Inquiry HC 947*. London: The Stationary Office.

Gollan PJ, Lewin D, Marchington M & Wilkinson A (2013) *Oxford Handbook of Participation in Organizations*. Oxford: Oxford University Press.

Green F (2004) Work intensification, discretion and the decline in well-being at work. *Eastern Economic Journal* 30(4):615–625.

House R (2016) Beyond the measurable: Alternatives to managed care in research and practice. In: Lees J (ed) *The Future of Psychological Therapy: From Managed Care to Transformational Practice*. London: Routledge, 146–164.

Jones RE (2010) *Foreshoring the Unconscious: Living Psychoanalytic Practice*. Medway: Layfield Press.

Larson E (2000) *Engaged Staff: What Do They Look Like and Why Might You Want Them*. London: The Good Work Commission.

Lupton D (2016) *The Quantified Self*. Cambridge: Polity Press.

Royal College of Nurses (2012) *RCN Labour Market Review: Overstretched: Under-Resourced*. London: Royal College of Nurses.

Standing G (2011) *The Precariat: The Dangerous New Underclass*. London: Palgrave Macmillan.

Taylor P, Cunningham I, Newsome K & Scholarios D (2010) "Too scared to go sick" – reformulating the research agenda on sickness absence. *Industrial Relations Journal* 41(4):270–288.

Trade Union Congress (2007) *Hard Work Hidden Lives: The Full Report of the Commission on Vulnerable Employment*. London: TUC.

Whitley R (1999) *Divergent Capitalisms: The Social Structuring and Change of Business Systems*. Oxford: Oxford University Press.

4 Precarious workers

"A lot of us who work in health have superegos the size of tanks. We've got this strong internal voice that says you must be right, do everything. Over time that can wear us down and make us very vulnerable to the external voices that say we should be ashamed for not being perfect."

Surviving work conversation: precarious workers

CHRIS: I'm not wishing to say we're trained badly, I think we're trained inadequately. I don't think we're prepared for the distress and the amount of work that's expected of most people going into healthcare. The distress that has to be held – the fact that it's recognised we need Schwartz rounds and Balint Groups. Psychotherapists, psychologists and psychiatrists can hold the distress they hold because they are in regular supervision. There is a lightening conductor for people working with distress in certain professions and not others, and that seems to me to be a big hole in how we treat doctors. We're now recommending self-care for the general public, and I think we now need self-care in the curriculum for doctors. We are wired firstly as people, not as doctors – these things become part of our being, they may be thrust upon us and part of expectations of our families, even before we're born.

CLARE: We're here in the Tavistock Clinic, which ran a whole series of seminars called Beyond Balint – run by Gerhard Wilke, who is a group analyst and anthropologist, and what he argues is that what general practice is now suffering from is the bereavement of the doctor-patient relationship being the most important relationship we can have in healthcare. Even that has fallen apart. We now have the 'third eye' in the consulting room – that's the commissioner. How much are you spending? Where are you referring patients? General practice has become both the scapegoat and saviour. Everything that's gone wrong in England is our fault – from climate change to the price of oranges. But we're also the saviours – GP led NHS, GPs running commissioning groups, go and see your GP. Being the saviour and the scapegoat does not sit well with individuals who just want to help their patients.

CHRIS: As if the job wasn't enough it's all the things doctors are expected to do around commissioning – being all things to all people and having all capabilities and competencies – nobody ever thinks about capacity. Part of this is increased patient expectations and the politicians who encourage those expectations and make the job impossible.

CLARE: But most of it is that there's no real interaction between us – patients and doctors, doctors and other doctors – it's the relationship between you and me that makes the difference.

CHRIS: I was a maladaptive perfectionist. I drove myself into the ground for the sake of my patients and my work. This is why I'm concerned that if we are deliberately selecting young people whose brains haven't even finished developing and putting them under high degrees of pressure – for doctors as a specific group of high achievers – I see this as a potentially major dark hole for people to enter. People self-pressurise, and unless we've got systems and measures in place for people to work safely there are going to be problems. It manifests itself in sickness absence, sickness presence, dysfunctional teams and patient experience, negligence claims and costs generally.

CLARE: It's trainees in hospitals that are in the worst state. This is because we treat training grade doctors as commodities. So they're there on a production line of care with no concept of them as a human being. For example, they might have a rota that is intolerable, changing daily, can you imagine what that does to your life? They also don't know where they're going to be long enough to get a lease on a property. They'll arrive in a hospital, and they'll be homeless. We don't provide them with sustenance any more – they might be on in the middle of the night and there's no hot food, just a vending machine. We imagine that they don't need continuity when we all need continuity. And then we expect them to show compassion. Come on.

CHRIS: This is one of the arguments about resilience. There are lots of resilient people around in this country, they're running it and running lots of people into the ground. I don't want resilience when I go and see a doctor, I want caring, and I want that person to be able to be healthy in themselves and supported. The greater the distress the more we need it. We can't hold other people if we're not in a position where we can hold ourselves.

To hear the full conversation with Chris Manning and Clare Gerada go to www.survivingworkinhealth.org.

Precarious workers

In 2016 the government announced a pilot programme to put job coaches into GP surgeries in Islington. This initiative came after years of independent reviews into disability assessments, attempts to put mental health services into job centres and complaints against the way in which fitness for work is assessed in the UK. A toxic combination of scripted assessments that do not take mental illness seriously, quotas for sanctions and the contracting out of the state's responsibility to protect vulnerable people.

The proposal to put job coaches into doctor's surgeries would be funny if you were not talking about actual human beings, including those who become the job coaches. The people who provide these new mental health services are, if the experience of the largest NHS programme, Increased Access to Psychological Therapies (IAPT), is anything to go by, likely to themselves be vulnerable. With low pay, limited training and low supervision the initiative raises the question of whether new job coaches will be able to contain their own anxieties, let alone those of their clients. Although I do not wish to be accused of negative thinking, is it possible that the people working in primary care are at risk of needing the support as much as the patients?

The vulnerability of an increasing number of health workers is a moral and strategic issue for our society made more pressing with the pressure for a 24/7 health service. NHS England chief executive Simon Stevens recently announced a £5 million scheme to improve the health of 1.3 million NHS workers. From healthy eating to fast-tracking mental health services this is an attempt to address a real problem.

Something that many of us missed was that this includes a specific health initiative for GPs. Doctors are increasingly vulnerable to burnout and depression – with particular groups such as trainee doctors and women GPs most vulnerable to suicide. But the data around the health of GPs is contested – not least because of the immense difficulties and shame attached to GPs admitting that they may not be able to make it all better for themselves.

There are systemic problems for GPs: the push for seven-day-week surgeries and the creation of the Clinical Commissioning Groups that hold the financial responsibilities of a broken system mean that frontline managers, often untrained to manage clinicians, are left having to juggle financial and clinical demands which cannot both be met.

The mental health of workers in primary care is a major cause for concern. A Mind research report in 2016 said that 88% of primary care workers find work stressful, leading 21% to develop associated mental health problems, most of whom are taking medication to deal with this. One in ten said that work stress had led them to have suicidal thoughts.

An indication of this pressure is that GP positions are getting harder to fill. In Scotland 20% of GP jobs remain unfilled – in an attempt to address this a £2 million training and recruitment fund has been created and in the short term a policy to recruit retired GPs into locum teams to cover on-call and weekend work. In preparation for a future crisis in replacing GPs after the mass of early retirements over the next five years, putting job coaches into GP surgeries is going to have to deliver for patients and doctors alike.

Research into the health of health workers is a source of great contention and involves more than a degree of irony. A 2015 survey of senior hospital doctors showed that 80% are considering early retirement just as the announcement landed that the doctors' union, the British Medical Association, had reluctantly agreed to negotiate compulsory weekend work for consultants.

As a result, state-funded positive thinking provokes a deeply cynical response from clinicians when there are attempts to build their collective 'resilience' through training designed to bolster their toughness, including the ability to 'bounce back' from adversity. As 74% of GPs say their workload is unmanageable the current suggestion that they might want to lay off the vino and go to Zumba may be met with some hostility.

Superheroes and superegos

Increasing numbers of reports on the mental health of clinicians are not about failures of individual compassion or positive thinking; rather they highlight the impact of precarious work on our states of mind. In particular the precarious states of mind that the kind of people who become doctors are vulnerable to.

It is a reality that in order to survive work we need defences. As a clinician you have to put on a psychic white robe and adopt a position where in the interests of the patient you have to do stuff that they do not want you to do. Putting it bluntly, a lot of medical treatment hurts and involves getting patients to do things they do not want to do. From heart medication to losing weight, 'The Doctor' sometimes has to know best and must have the authority to defend that position with the patient.

We want them to be authoritative and have all the answers – where they are able to diagnose the tumour, remove it and cure us. But we also want them to do a more delicate job of healing our minds and bodies which are always involved in the process of getting better. This is a delicate procedure requiring sensitivity, diplomacy and a big dose of humanity.

There is something about GPs that makes them vulnerable. The nature of the training means the career attracts people who make massive demands on themselves – an internal script of 'do this now' rather than 'what can I realistically do?' For many, medical training is an entry into the cult of perfection where massively bright people become highly vulnerable to fantasies of omnipotence. This might explain why one-third of all doctors say they would not raise their own mental distress with colleagues because of the shame they would feel and the potential for career damage.

At the same time, a doctor cannot always be 'emotionally defended', where they adopt psychological strategies to defend themselves from the pain and anxiety they are exposed to. Dealing with distress is distressing – and increasingly so on the primary care frontline. People are coming to GP surgeries with more severe health problems and higher levels of mental distress in part because of the cuts in long-term services and public services that previously would have helped people step away from the cliff edge.

Exposure to psychological risk is inevitably part of the job, but some coping strategies could result in doctors losing their curiosity and compassion towards their patients. By being cut off from patients, real problems can be missed. This is particularly the case with mental health where the psychosomatic complaints we innocently take to our GPs are sometimes code for distress. Medically unexplained symptoms and the 30% of UK adults with temporomandibular disorders (TMD) should raise curiosity in the scientist's mind but are often fobbed off with painkillers.

It takes a real human being to spot the human in others, so health and social care workers have to be defended enough to treat the patient even when it hurts but not allow those defences to become so brittle that they cease to care.

It means that the optimum situation is that health and social care workers can shift their roles and ways of working within every working day. The ideal healthcare worker is robust enough to treat a patient who doesn't want to hear it and emotionally engaged enough to actually listen to the patient who does not know what is wrong.

Feeling like a failure

This sense of failure is actively encouraged by the demands for certainty, treatment and targets now expected of GPs. There is no room within this system for 'not knowing' what is wrong or any sense that both the clinician and patient can take the time to do the detective work of reaching a diagnosis and finding the right treatment. With five minute appointments it's not hard to explain the medicalisation of distress in the UK.

I do not wish to appear rude, but doctors are highly competitive and sometimes just a bit narcissistic, meaning that their expectation is that somehow they can achieve whatever targets or quotas are being set. For many doctors the realities of working in primary care are pretty disappointing. No longer a superhero in the making, just holding together a very bad public health situation. Grieving this heroic model of care is not easy because it involves tackling a range of defences against pain including insisting that you are OK when you very much are not.

It should not be necessary to remind health workers this, but there is something strangely difficult about admitting that life is impossible without other people and acting accordingly. Perhaps it is cultural (how *gauche* to admit I need you) and cuts against our prized independence and individualism (what? I'm nothing without *you*?). Whatever the causes, it is also dangerous because it upsets the conservative order of things where friends and family are your concern and everyone else is not. It is less of a headache to see your interests as connected only to people you love rather than to be burdened by things like public services or maintaining real social networks.

Sadly, romantic ideas about love conquering all are tested to the extreme during an economic crisis. Feelings get stirred up – often rather unattractive ones like irritation and anger. These emotions may be triggered because someone reliable has become unreliable, upsetting the status quo and reversing roles within relationships. Relationships break down not just because of hard financial realities but facing the psychic realities that people we like can disappoint us, particularly at work.

There is something deeply anti-relationship about many people's reactions to threat, often a very real sense of 'fight or flight'. Adrenaline shoots through our veins, and fists start forming. At this point if your sense of being rooted in your workplace or your relationships is weak, the obvious reaction is to run. This retreat into flight is fundamentally rejecting, leaving behind people, organisations and careers that have often been built up over years.

The majority of these flights, though, are internal, resulting in a retreat from contact with others. We are more than capable of resentfully wheeling out the statement 'I stayed, didn't I?' but actually living in a mental bunker that cuts us off from others and, therefore, reality. This predictable, assured and relatively secure psychic reality is a delusion because it says that only I can sort out my own problems. Because it is a delusion, it comes at the expense of living in the real world where we are dependent on the care of other people and, if you want to get hippy about it, a benevolent universe.

One of the reasons for this dependency is that it's through our relationships with others that we actually know anything about ourselves.

Although it is no longer considered eccentric to think that there are parts of our minds that function at the unconscious level, it is surprising how little health workers refer to the unconscious in our daily work. The problem with raising the issue of the unconscious might be something to do with the annoying fact that we have little awareness of our own unconscious precisely because it is, well, unconscious.

Freud originally came from a neurology background and spent his working life trying to understand the workings of the mind, including the presence of an unconscious and how we can access it. Freud saw these as unfulfilled instinctual wishes that the conscious mind finds unacceptable, known through dreams, slips and free association. His view, and the basis for talking therapies, is that we need other people to pick up on the signs and signals of the unconscious. The process of psychoanalysis involves listening to what the unconscious mind is trying to communicate, despite the best efforts of the conscious mind. The point of this is to help people understand how they really feel and bring these feelings into consciousness in order to make steps towards acceptance and sometimes change.

This implies the even more controversial point that other people might be able to see the workings of our unconscious minds more clearly than we do. This is rather unsettling and explains why being stuck in a lift with a psychoanalyst could make you a bit paranoid.

Protecting yourself

Honestly, it is a bit cheeky to make suggestions to doctors about improving their health, but here goes. Based on the experience of people working in healthcare, here are some initial steps towards protecting yourself at work.

Like most things your doctor tells you, doing it is a lot harder than it sounds, and you might feel vaguely irritated at the simplicity of the ideas. This is absolutely OK because the reality is that we like to think we are more sophisticated and unique than we actually are and that the commonality of our experiences at work allows us to say some general things about how to protect ourselves at work.

1. Start where you are

When it comes to surviving work we first have to be clear what the problem is. On an individual level this means taking a look at where we really are in life.

This sounds obvious in the cold light of day, but a very human defence against disappointment is to pretend that things are better than they are. One of the reasons for this is that it requires admitting that you are an ordinary human being who sometimes feels vulnerable and does not always have a solution.

Being an ordinary human being often cuts against our culture, particularly in healthcare where the pressure is on to always do more work and not make mistakes. Although this is impossible to achieve it is an important motivator and driver within clinical work and is something we have to overcome if we want to get a realistic idea of where we really are in life.

The second difficulty in facing up to where you are in life is that it often means you have to confront difficult emotions, such as anger. This is a tricky one for clinicians because although we might be very good at dealing with other people's emotions, it's much harder to confront our own. Some of us can feel humiliated that we experience the same problems as our patients.

Most workplaces are also very demanding about how we communicate – with some taboos about showing emotion, particularly negative ones. However, in order to really understand our own states of mind we have to be able to look honestly at how we feel.

2. Setting your limits

The second important stage of protecting yourself is to set some boundaries for yourself about when and how you work. Establishing a sustainable way of working requires being realistic and accepting that you cannot do everything. Again, it is important to show yourself some compassion here, rather than listening to an internal voice which can bully you into doing the right thing when it is not right for you.

Setting limits can also mean disagreeing with a workplace culture that does not tolerate limitations. Although being human means accepting that we are not superheroes, it is a surprisingly difficult thing to get your head around. This is compounded by some workplaces having a 'sink or swim' mentality with the 'ideal' doctors fighting fires, saving lives and changing the world.

Although there is a real need for health and social care workers to be resilient, this toughness is not a substitute for good mental health because it denies the hard realities of time, resources and emotional limitations.

Standing up for yourself is hard and can evoke real anxiety and locking yourself in the toilets. Although it might not feel as if you have any control over your anxiety levels, it is important to take some initial steps to calm yourself down before trying to work out what to do next. First aid, an initial response to a problem, takes a very simple and useful approach to take some immediate control over your anxiety, and you could use a five-stage approach to this that can be called CABIN (nice mental picture of a safe place in a wood, birds and Bambi).

> **Contain:** Remove yourself from whatever is making you anxious and find somewhere where you feel safe. If you can call a friend or find someone at work you trust to help you.
>
> **Acknowledge:** Do not try to ignore what has just happened. Acknowledge the anxiety you are feeling.
>
> **Breathe:** Try to control your breathing, lengthening your breath, and if it helps count one-two-three slowly in your head. Keep going until your breathing has normalised.
>
> **Identify:** Work out what you are worried about right now.
>
> **Next steps:** Work out what the next steps should be. This stage is always better if you can find a friend to do this with.

Probably the most effective way of reducing anxiety is to contact a friend or someone you trust at work and ask them to help you. When you are anxious you are unlikely to be thinking straight so find a time when you are relatively relaxed and think through who you would call and make sure you have their number on your phone.

If someone comes to you with a problem that is making them anxious it is important to let them speak and to listen without interrupting or correcting them. On one level anxiety is a problem of misperceiving reality, but by pointing out the facts of the matter you are unlikely to help anyone feel less anxious. What is important is that you acknowledge they are feeling anxious and gently help them think about what they can do next.

The main point here is that it is unavoidable that at some point you will need to stand up to unrealistic demands and to stand firm on what you believe is a sustainable framework for you. This might involve setting a time limit for responding to emails, keeping your private number private and being explicit about tasks or areas of work that you are not comfortable doing. It might not make you popular, but it will help you survive work.

3. A protective approach

Most of us have a mixture of risks and protective factors in our lives, and central to a protective approach is being able to identify what they are and how to manage them. Some things are not easily changed, such as disability or housing, but other factors we can influence to reduce our risks and increase our protective factors.

We all have habits and behaviours that undermine our capacity to stand up for ourselves, doctors included, and whatever your view of the systemic causes of bullying these will need to be addressed as well.

Some of the most obvious and difficult risk factors are toxic coping strategies, which can range from using alcohol or drugs to burying ourselves in work. Addictions function to help us cut off emotionally as a way of managing anxiety. It means that we become numbed to what is happening around us and internally.

All of us at certain points need to have coping mechanisms and things we can rely on to help us deal with anxiety and the pain that it causes. This is particularly the case with overwork, which most people do not address because it is a 'socially acceptable' defence and often encouraged by workplace cultures.

However, inherent in toxic coping strategies is a paradox in that they actually make us less able to cope over time because they undermine our self-confidence. Addiction involves a series of blackmails that if you challenge the dependency then you risk losing everything, or at least that is how it feels.

What we do know is that unless we tackle our toxic coping strategies things are likely to get worse so a key part of protecting yourself is going to be finding people and services that can help you overcome any addictions that you have.

4. Next steps

Consciously knowing about and addressing our risks and protective factors is an essential part of protecting ourselves because it is on the basis of what we really know about ourselves and our environments that we can adopt some meaningful ways to improve our situation at work.

Probably the most helpful advice will be from people who are experiencing the same issues as you, and there is a list of some places you can start in Chapter 9. Over 75,000 health workers use Twitter, so there are many additional resources and campaigns online which you might find helpful in establishing your next steps.

An ordinary experience of actually surviving work in healthcare is worth its weight in gold, so go find it.

5. Having someone you can rely on

Getting help is probably the most important factor in surviving the experience of work. This is difficult for everyone, principally for two reasons. The first is that it means admitting that there is a problem you cannot fix alone. Most people working in health will find it difficult to reach out to other people because it is something we do not normally do. Additionally, not coping at work can leave us feeling isolated and alone, making it a huge effort to articulate a problem to someone else. When you need help the most you are least likely to feel like asking for it.

The second issue is finding the right person or people to help you. The selection of people or organisations is important because they need to be people we trust and think are on our side. Although most people would like to call on their family and close friends, sometimes it can be difficult to know whom you can go to.

Sometimes, help comes from people we may not immediately think of. It is important to think about people you have relied on in the past and what specific help at work you need. Often these people can be colleagues, and it is important not to discount asking for help just because you are not closely connected on an emotional level.

Trade unions are central to protecting members – as the largest membership organisations in the world their experience of handling difficult situations at work is unparalleled. There are over 200,000 trade union representatives in the UK, ranging from elected leaders to paid officials to lay representatives. All of them deal with the daily realities of conflict, redundancies, grievances and the increasing crisis of mental health at work. A good place to start to look for support would be to contact your local union representative – if they do not phone you back in five minutes, phone again, and again if you have to. Do not be put off by the fact that, as with doctors, reps are caught in a supply versus demand situation when it comes to human distress.

The main thing is to make sure you take the important step of enlisting others to help you because it radically increases your likelihood of surviving work. You can do this informally or look to establish a formal mentoring relationship or make use of your professional memberships. However you structure this, it is important to work out whom you think you can rely on and talk to them about your situation before the crisis hits. In the main, people respond well to requests for help and often are flattered to be considered a friend.

6. Survival is an ongoing process

There is no one-fix measure for surviving work because the key is about our capacities for adapting to change. This means that, by its nature, surviving work is a process of knowing where we really are, managing our risks and protective factors and being realistic about what we can do for ourselves and other people. We should not feel like failures because of the reality that we have to keep addressing our capacity to survive work throughout our careers.

7. How we treat each other matters

It is now a national sport to develop what has become known as 'social capital'. For the non-capitalists amongst you that means relationships with other people.

Most people want to get on with the people around them but find it very difficult to do. Especially during restructuring and when hierarchical systems of management are in place, it is difficult to maintain good communications even within our own teams.

In mental health, clinicians often make use of clinical supervision groups, where small groups of clinicians meet on a regular basis to discuss cases and their experiences of them. These groups are usually facilitated by a senior clinician, and each member takes a turn to present cases and critical incidents to the group. Clinical supervision groups are crucial to maintaining communication between teams and also for building team working. There are models of running supervision groups which emphasise the emotional and psychological impact of dealing with cases, predominantly used in psychotherapeutic and psychoanalytic settings.

In a conversation we recorded about the working lives of GPs we talked to Clare Gerada, who is a GP and works with the NHS Practitioner Health Programme, and Chris Manning from Action for NHS Wellbeing, a network that works for a healthy workforce. These people are of the brave and humane variety – willing to talk about their own states of mind and at the same time possessing the brass to shout loud at policy and committee meetings where talking about depression and burnout is received like a fart in a lift. Both organisations offer support to individuals, but more importantly, they offer an invitation to GPs to form relationships with each other where the reality of their situations can be known without shame.

The existence of practitioner networks – whether at the level of professional bodies, unions, support groups like these or online networks – is not just of therapeutic importance, it's also of political importance. Because until health and social care workers can openly challenge this system of impossible targets, they cannot establish a profession worthy of them. This means moving beyond the individual towards developing relationships with the people we work with that are sufficiently strong to challenge the demands being placed on us.

The new occupational health scheme for health workers is a potential opportunity, but as the crisis deepens, how we treat each other matters more. If you are struggling to survive work this week and you feel like packing your psychic bags, don't. Instead, take the risk and tell someone that you need their help.

Reading

Armstrong D (2005) *Organisation in the Mind: Psychoanalysis, Group Relations, and Organizational Consultancy*. London: Karnac.

Britton R (2003) *Sex, Death, and the Superego: Experiences in Psychoanalysis*. London: Karnac Books.

Cortina M & Marrone M (Eds) (2002) *Attachment Theory and the Psychoanalytic Process*. London: Whurr Publishers.

Dolan P (2014) *Happiness by Design: Finding Pleasure and Purpose in Everyday Life*. London: Penguin Books.

Fonagy P (1994) The Emmanuel Miller memorial lecture 1992: The theory and practice of resilience (with M Steele, H Steele, A Higgitt, and M Target). *Journal of Child Psychology and Psychiatry and Allied Disciplines* 35:231–257.

Grant L & Kinman G (2014) *Developing Resilience for Social Work Practice*. London: Palgrave.

Hammond P (2015) *Staying Alive: How to Get the Best from the NHS*. London: Quercus Publishing.

HMG (2008) *Working for a Healthier Tomorrow: Dame Carol Black's Review of the Health of Britain's Working Age Population*. London: TSO.

Layard R, Bell S, Clark DM, Knapp M, Meacher M & Priebe S (2006) *The Depression Report: A New Deal for Depression and Anxiety Disorders*. London: London School of Economics.

Lees J (2016) (Ed) *The Future of Psychological Therapy: From Managed Care to Transformational Practice*. London: Routledge.

Mental Health Taskforce (2016) *Five Year Forward View for Mental Health*. London: Mental Health Taskforce.

Moloney P (2013) *The Therapy Industry: The Irresistible Rise of the Talking Cure, and Why It Doesn't Work*. London: Pluto Press.

Smail D (2005) *Power Interest and Psychology: Elements of a Social Materialist Understanding of Distress*. Ross-on-Wye: PCCS Books.

Thornicroft G (2006) *Actions Speak Louder . . . Tackling Discrimination against People with Mental Illness*. London: Mental Health Foundation.

5 Walk the line

"The response to whistleblowers – shooting the messenger – is about what happens when people find that their 'not-knowing' is challenged. One of the responses is to become forceful in blocking unwelcome knowledge."

Surviving work conversation: walk the line

ROGER: On everything else apart from racism the NHS is run on data. You've got an MRSA outbreak on a ward – you look at the data, talk to the staff, look elsewhere in the organisation to see how they've dealt with it and set up a learning loop. Since race discrimination is bad for patient care, you have to do the same. Start with the data, listen to the staff and that's the start of the conversation. For a lot of organisations they have had to look at data that's very uncomfortable to look at. If you're in a large teaching hospital where it's four times more likely that BME [black and minority ethnic] staff will be disciplined than white staff, you can't change those numbers without understanding why it's happening.

CORREEN: It's all about power. If you're in a leadership role and you don't understand culturally what's happening, it can be interpreted in lots of different ways. BME staff often become that person, you become the whistleblower, you become the 'sensitive' person who is always accusing other people of racism. I can see that in a community of other professionals you can confirm that experience because generally that's not the way that most people are thinking.

ROGER: There's data that shows on average black and minority ethnic staff who go for jobs are better qualified than white staff. We have people on Band 6 and 7 with master's in business administration who say, 'I can't get a job in the NHS'. Well, actually, the MBA isn't the way to get the job. You've only done the MBA because to some degree you know you're good, you weren't recognised in the way that other people were so you think, 'Right, I'll go and do another qualification'. But actually the reason you didn't get the job was because you weren't part of the club. No number of qualifications will get you into the club until the rules of the club change.

CORREEN: I'm curious if we think of this idea of an internal bully, just how many black and minority ethnic people that get told as they grow up that to achieve anything you have to be better. So for someone to come directly and challenge you and say, 'You're not better', actually that voice is already inside you.

ROGER: People who are being bullied can eventually start to think, 'Well, maybe it's me'. It's common for whistleblowers that once the retaliation takes the form of bullying they start to think, 'Well, maybe I'm not such a good worker after all'. Even though all their previous records will show generally they are exemplary employees, which is probably why they became a whistleblower because they wouldn't tolerate poor practice.

CORREEN: On an individual level the way to defend against racism is to trust your instincts and to recognise that what is happening is actually happening. You disbelieve yourself – surely this isn't what's happening? Then you have to start to find a safe way to try to expose it, recognising it's risky, it's always risky because the fear is that you're not going to be believed. So believing in yourself is a good starting point. Then finding people who you can trust to tell you the truth – bearing in mind that some people will always feed into any drama that's going on, but you have to find people you trust.

To hear the full conversation with Roger Kline and Correen Archer go to www.survivingworkinhealth.org.

Walk the line

Sometimes working in healthcare forces you to walk a very thin line between the personal and the political – an awkward place somewhere between the consulting room, Whitehall and the boardroom. The advantage of being in the business of caring for real human beings is that most of us have to live in the real world far from the neurolinguistic programming and misinformation that dominates in the debates about the healthcare. There is plenty of scope in the current political climate to say something that has actual meaning.

It means that health workers can often trump politicians by speaking about things that are true – the real costs of care and what we risk if we walk away from the psychic realities of living with economic decline.

The capacity to speak authentically is still high currency amongst human beings, and many politically active clinicians do well on social media for that reason. Some would argue that the growing political engagement of people working in health has become essential to protecting patient care.

But it also presents us with a dilemma about when our capacity to articulate truths which are hard to hear becomes a belief in magic wands, superheroes and our own power to change things. Cure the patient becomes cure the NHS and then cure the world.

One of the advantages of working in healthcare is that it forces you to be humble. No point in pretending that we are not all human beings who get ill and have limitations when your job is to help people recover. Omnipotence, certainty and absolute clarity are beaten up in the toilets of the mind, leaving you a bigger person but probably not very good at glossing over the truth and maintaining your enthusiasm for yet another public health policy shift.

However, it might be that this humility allows us to walk an important line where we are able to say things that are true but also listen to other people. To allow ourselves to take a position but be influenced by what the people around us have to say. To question the political facts, including our own.

If the entire history of improving working conditions through collective action is anything to go by, this involves setting the battle lines – the principles that form the basis of care – and the conditions under which those principles can survive. The over-emphasis on what needs to be delivered for less money comes at the expense of doing this. This political deficit in shaping healthcare in the UK means that a central task for all of us, whether patients or clinicians, is to take a position on the values that underpin the NHS and to defend them.

This is both a political and concrete task: to defend a principle of care that is fair both to patients and staff, and to build sufficiently strong relationships with the people we work with where we can work responsively rather than defensively.

The question, of course, is how. All of us struggle to build relationships given the common and powerful reasons why it is so very hard to make friends and influence people at work. The proposal of this section is that it requires us to walk a number of lines – between saying nothing and whistleblowing, between getting angry enough to change things but not so angry you lose your job, between being pessimistic and optimistic and between the ping pong between love and hate we experience with the people we work closely with.

Between saying nothing and whistleblowing

The third Francis report on how to build a safe NHS focussed on the problem of how staff can raise their concerns about patient care without fear of victimisation or whistleblowing – a last resort that happens only when there are no other adequate avenues to report failures.

The report, which took evidence from more than 600 people about their experiences in the NHS and another 19,000 from an online survey, says nothing new to those working in the NHS, where bullying is recognised to be endemic and where most people survive working in the NHS by keeping their mouths shut.

The report tries to get to the bottom of this bullying crisis by going to the real experts, the people working in the NHS. Hardly a radical idea, but chronically missing in an institution dominated by top-down targets and feverish policy-level action, all of which has totally and utterly ignored the working realities of the people who are supposed to deliver them.

As a result, there is important stuff in the report about the reality of working in healthcare. I don't wish to over complicate things here, but there are some really bad jobs in the NHS. In an attempt to save costs, the way people work in the NHS has changed, with a radical increase in temporary and agency work, outsourcing, zero hours contracts and work intensification and a decline in real wages.

These changes in the employment relationship have triggered changes in the duty of care towards patients, including projecting risks and duties away from the principal employer onto service providers and labour agencies. And the negative impact on patient safety of these trends is a growing theme in both clinical and employment relations research.

Along with the revival of discrimination and racism, and the emergence of command and control management, it is no wonder that most NHS staff feel too vulnerable to speak up.

Tied into the debates about compassionate care is the duty of care, a complex mix of rules and regulations that apply to NHS staff. Every health and social care professional and manager is responsible for legal duties of care, including professional codes, articulated in the newly amended NHS Constitution. It means that people working in health and social care have a personal duty of care to provide good clinical care and with it a duty of candour to raise concerns about poor practice.

This is acknowledged in the government's response to the Morecambe Bay investigation and the recent Freedom to Speak Up recommendations which include establishing a system of guardians to encourage people to, unsurprisingly, speak up.

The problem continues to be the severe limitations of a purely regulatory system that does not address the real reasons why people are not raising their concerns.

In first place is the fear of victimisation from colleagues and employers. The Freedom to Speak Up review concluded that in order to get people to speak up, the blame culture in the NHS needs to be addressed. This problem is often framed as the need to make the shift to a 'just culture' – one that makes a distinction between at-risk or reckless behaviour and simple human error. A working culture that looks systemically at care, rather than taking the witch hunt school of management which individualises collective problems.

The argument is that although regulation is important, if the response to mistakes and poor practice is to blame and penalise clinicians, staff will not be willing to come forward.

It means that those people who do raise their concerns can, whatever the rights and wrongs of the situation, become deeply resented and isolated within teams. Many find themselves completely unsupported by colleagues, who fear a Pandora's box situation being triggered. This reluctance to support and work with people when they raise concerns raises the odds of whistleblowing. As a team's resistance to looking at problems deepens, the volume of the whistle goes up.

It also explains the viciousness that many whistleblowers face from colleagues. In workplaces where staff are silenced there is likely to be an intense fear of people who speak up and present the case for change. As a defence against anxiety, it is much easier to bully a guardian into silence through a ruthless wall of non-cooperation than to address the systemic problems of why they are needed in the first place. Shoot the messenger and with it you lose the opportunity to address issues around patient care.

You seem angry, are you angry?

Probably the most common and least acceptable feeling at work is anger. The trouble with anger is that it is an ugly emotion. When you are going through a problem at work, probably the most consistent piece of 'advice' offered is do not, whatever you do, get angry. When you are actually angry this is less helpful than you imagine, underlining the profound difference between advice and help, the latter being a rare thing and the former given in abundance, especially from a position of relative security. The thing about telling an angry person not to get angry is that it is something of a vicious circle. You are angry, a demand is made that you calm down and regulate your feelings, you feel this denies the legitimacy of why you are angry and you get more angry, even harder to calm down.

For a start there is a lot to get angry about. Our work and the value of it are seriously threatened in the current public services climate. To those of us witnessing a devaluing of our contribution and experience, the public sector ethos now sounds like something from the 1950s. The difficulty, though, with getting angry is how to direct it at the right things.

Working with distress is distressing – other people's confusion, pain and challenging behaviour affect us, and this often evokes anger. A very common way for health workers to deal with this uncomfortable human reality is to direct this anger not at the patient but with colleagues. This is not just about being left out of staff football or after-work drinks; it includes scapegoating, vindictive behaviour and even violence. In my work with teams in the NHS I have learned always to clarify when people talk about violence at work whether they are talking about patients or, as is more common, co-workers.

It is a very difficult aspect for us to accept that often our reaction to people who are clearly struggling at work can be one of revulsion and rejection, even anger. In psychoanalysis we often think about this as a process of projection, where people try to rid themselves of their own angry and aggressive feelings by projecting them into the people around them.

If you are someone suffering from mental health problems you can often present an ideal receptacle for other people's projections – 'she's the crazy lady, not me!' In times of recession this rapid process of projection looks more like an Olympic ping pong match. The anger directed at people who are already struggling to regulate their feelings easily spills over into actual violence.

Anger is often misunderstood as a character failing rather than an emotion linked closely to fear. Often, particularly for men, fear becomes anger very quickly. A report, *Delivering Male*, by the National Mental Health Development Unit explains the additional difficulties that men have in disclosing depression and reports that their symptoms can sometimes be unexpectedly angry, such as aggressive behaviour and getting really, really drunk. Just because someone is frightening you it does not mean that they themselves are not frightened. And the problems get worse in the workplace where we are not supposed to admit to being afraid or vulnerable; rather we tend to exhibit more aggressive and assertive characteristics. No wonder then that there are so many angry people at work.

Under these pressures it is important to acknowledge the strengths of our feelings towards our own and other peoples' states of minds. The reality of anger at work is one explanation for the massive growth in mindfulness at work, a meditation 'lite' technique to manage stress. This is a technique taken from religious worship and practice but adapted to workplace and more general secular application.

Mindfulness techniques encourage slower and deeper breathing, which can effectively reduce our heart rates and blood pressure. Research indicates that mindfulness techniques can build our immune systems as well. Neurological research indicates that mindfulness techniques effect the pre-frontal cortex where the left brain became stronger, indicating increased positive mood, and the insula, the part of the brain responsible for feelings of empathy, also becomes more active.

Some people benefit from building their capacity to get into a reflective state when under pressure. Although when we are angry being told to calm down can be deeply unhelpful and often very difficult to do, the argument is that this more calm conscious awareness allows for less reactive and more intentional states, including acknowledging how we feel, accepting things as they are and building a sense of what might be a healthy way forward rather than a rush into action.

Personally, for me it took ten years of psychic warfare and retreats to monasteries in Nepal to come within a million miles of a meditation. At one point when I was setting up Surviving Work I tried to raise money to produce an app – entitled 'No Punching or Spitting', just to give you an idea of my internal script, purely coincidentally during a period when I was in a compulsory redundancy pool. I had come to believe that mindfulness was a conspiracy to silence me – compounded by my experience that the most vicious and attacking responses to my writing about anger came from Buddhists. I am not having a pop at the Dalai Lama, but I would like to suggest that in my experience many people who train with such devotion to manage their feelings start out from a pretty angry place.

As someone who is naturally very angry it was not until I could, in that age-old cliché, 'own' my anger that I could develop a relationship with it. In reality, once I accepted that I was actually angry, and pretty good at it too, it became possible for me to find techniques that would allow me to turn the volume down long enough to channel this anger into something that was actually worth getting angry about. A kind of mindful anger. What I have never been convinced by is the denial of the obvious fact that everybody, including the devoted mindfulness practitioner, can get angry and that increasingly this is an occupational hazard.

So given that there is a lot of anger around in healthcare, what could be a healthy attitude towards it? It might lie in the understanding that anger is necessary to the process of change. The energy and focus that you have when you are angry are important motivators in challenging things that we think are wrong, in my case a rather priggish attachment to fairness.

I also think it is one of the most important reasons why some people experience depression and others do not. If you can get angry you are really living, really experiencing and reacting to what is going on around you. Depression is a numbing and dumbing process to try to avoid feelings of sadness and anger. And it is precisely this that makes depression essentially an experience of hopelessness.

So this is why I am all in favour of anger – because of its relationship to the future. If you are angry, you are also hopeful that things should and could change. The trick is to manage and direct this anger, rather than allow it to spill over into conflict at work. So however we do this – by walking out of a room to calm down, meditating or just making sure you do not swear at your manager – we all need to calm down just enough to be able to focus our anger onto a problem that truly deserves it.

You're being very negative

In 2016 I joined 1,000 people at an event in London to listen to the daddy of positive psychology, Martin Seligman. Definitely not my usual tribe, but I went to dip my toe into the dominant model for workplace wellbeing as research for this book. The last time I went on an optimism course I was asked to leave because of my ruthless pessimism and stubborn references to the human condition – but I felt enough time and therapy had passed for me to try to play nicely with the other more positive children.

The event kicked off with a fake listening exercise: think back to the last week about something positive that happened and tell the person next to you. I was stuck with a twenty-six-year-old positive psychologist who talked about her boyfriend's BBQ that weekend. I could hardly open my mouth thinking of the young black man I had talked down from jumping in front of a tube train while about thirty people on the platform literally looked the other way. I squeezed something out about being grateful for being able to be more open with my friends about how I am struggling. She thought I had not understood the question.

Despite the growth of the 'wellbeing' industry in the UK, there are currently no national guidelines or consensus amongst practitioners on how to build wellbeing at work. Workplace wellbeing programmes tend to be based on a model of positive psychology which is based on a cognitive behavioural therapy (CBT) model. Using this model, Martin Seligman set up the influential PENN Resilience Programme (PRP) and established a model of positive psychology for schools and workplaces. A range of 'resilience' and 'happiness' initiatives have sprung up from Seligman's research such as Action for Happiness, founded by Richard Layard with the Dalai Lama their high-profile patron. The principal exception to this positive psychology model has been an initiative called Mental Health First Aid, delivered by the mental health charity Rethink, which gives awareness-raising training on mental illness and practical guidance on how to manage distress at work.

Before we go any further I would like to say that I do not hate positivity or CBT. I do, however, have an issue with the hubris around positive psychology and how it gets used by ideologically driven governments and patronising employers to punish people with problems at work. The spread of positive psychology is also a story of power and money. It is cheap, and if it does not work it leaves the individual carrying the systemic failure that promotes positive thinking as a long-term response to social crisis.

There has been a lot of research about optimism and how to develop more optimistic patterns in life. This is based on the view that if we believe that a positive outcome can happen it raises the possibility that it will happen. Optimism is defined as expecting the future to be better than history predicts where, unlike a completely realistic or slightly pessimistic view, there is a difference between expectations and outcomes. The optimism argument is that those people who have an optimistic expectation are more likely to have positive outcomes because it alters our perception of reality and so provides an essential confidence and motivation to reach our goals.

Although neuroscience does not give us a complete picture of why some people are more optimistic than others (and let's face it, most of us are not neuroscientists), it does indicate that thinking and feeling positive has an impact on the brain. If you must know, imagining positive future events shows higher brain activity in the amygdala (bit of the brain that processes emotion) and the rostral anterior cingulate cortex (rACC), which regulates the connection between emotion and motivation, the 'traffic conductor' enhancing the flow of positive emotion. The conclusions that are drawn from this include ones which might seem intuitively right, including that if we believe there will be a positive outcome, it is more likely to happen.

Seligman's research argues that our optimism is shaped by an internal script or explanatory style which is a way of thinking about causes. Positive psychology uses exercises that quickly stimulate positive thought patterns and behaviours, often with an emphasis on identifying individual 'strengths', challenging negative thinking and promoting 'positive' alternative scripts. Activities attempt to challenge internal 'negative' scripts or patterns of thought by asking participants to create alternative positive scripts. This process attempts to reduce feelings of anxiety and low mood by helping individuals 'de-catastrophise' their emotions and experiences.

One of the main problems with using positive psychology in workplaces is that it under-emphasises the impact of external factors on individual wellbeing and regards the work of building wellbeing as essentially one of addressing the symptoms rather than the causes. Its attraction is that it promotes the idea that optimism can be learned through a set of skills and behaviours that can quickly improve individual states of mind. The widespread use of positive psychology techniques is due, in part, to their simplicity and usability but also the economic argument for short-term interventions developed by Layard, rather than tackling systemic workplace problems.

Although self-regulation techniques are useful, they do not work if the emotion itself is suppressed. In a context of job insecurity, victimisation and workplace bullying, being told to focus on positive thoughts and breathing exercises can be highly provocative in that it denies the significance of what can go wrong at work and provides a relatively weak response to feelings of anger and hopelessness.

Trades unions, as well as some psychosocial schools of psychology, are critical of this model of wellbeing for obscuring important external economic and political realities. From a trade union perspective, workplace attempts to 'engage' employees through wellbeing programmes are often viewed with some scepticism and as a way of controlling and depoliticising worker demands for material changes. This rejection of wellbeing and, more recently, 'resilience' agendas rests on positive psychology's emphasis on individual cognitions and behaviours, which under-emphasises external factors – such as precarious working conditions or lack of social capital – which have an important impact on wellbeing.

One of the problems with workplace wellbeing schemes is that they can easily look like a social realism campaign. Your workplace needs you! Eat breakfast and you can produce twice as many widgets for the empire! I am not against breakfast or fruit, but what we do know is that 'nanny' messaging by employers has at best no impact and at worst a negative effect because it removes our reliance on our internal capacities. Promoting psychological wellbeing goes against, for example, the principles of adult education promoted in this book, which highlight making a realistic assessment of the root problem and collective problem solving.

Positive psychology's potential lack of realism goes some way to explain why for many of us there is something strangely disempowering about many of these schemes. I call this the positivity paradox. Once a woman came to see me about taking a course I run on surviving work. She asked me if the fact that she had lost her job three months ago meant that she was no longer eligible. This woman is an expert in survival, but she thought she had already failed.

This is where I think many of us have to walk the wellbeing line at work – to engage with positive behaviours enough to make us feel better(ish) rather than a wholesale rejection of feeling OK but to not over-state what wellbeing initiatives can do to help us survive work in the long term. Although feeling positive about work at least some of the time is essential, this cannot be done on the basis of suppressing our real feelings and experiences of work. Wellbeing at work is only really possible if it does not make us feel good about working conditions that are actually bad for us.

Between love and hate

One of the problems with the current marketised and legalised model of care is that it creates splits – between colleagues and between staff and patients – and de-emphasises the important duty of care that staff have to each other. The reality is that if we are to improve clinical practice, staff have to be able to form relationships that are strong enough to manage difficult conversations about the mistakes and unfair choices that are inherent in the job.

In this highly politicised healthcare system the duty of care debate is dominated by clinicians' responsibilities to their patients. This is not to suggest that patients are not at the heart of the NHS, but to do this at the expense of the other duties involved in care has turned out to be a disaster.

Against a marketised model of care (I sell stuff, you buy it) stands a relational model of care where our relationships with each other – with patients and between staff – take priority in the design of services.

Many of us are highly active in organising and team building on the front line. There is a kind of begrudging love between many of us who share a profession, a shared idea of professionalism or the agape of 'brotherly love'. This love is close to the Greek word 'philia', a friendly love but with a generous pinch of the caring familial love of storage and passionate Eros.

The way that work in healthcare is organised is also the source of loving bonds between groups of healthcare workers – late night chats and small group discussions where people ask each other what they think and actually listen to the answers. Good team builders seduce people into a powerful sense of belonging, where they can generalise about their connectedness and be part of the bigger picture. For many people joining a profession offers this sense of belonging, a workplace equivalent of secure attachment and the primary basis for surviving work.

Getting on with people at work can build what Turquet calls 'oneness' – a strange, almost cellular connection between people. Something like the Greek idea of storage, the begrudging love you have for a younger sibling who irritates and inspires at exactly the same time, locked together in a 'union' against a common enemy, whether it is parents, austerity or patients. In this sense teams are often prone to paranoia, where 'fear simplifies the emotional situation'. Them and Us.

This familial love is essential for understanding the pressures healthcare workers put each other under, which from the outside look like the stuff of abusive relationships. Continual demands for a sacrificial offering and relentless calls on free time and emotional energy for the greater good. Shift patterns that move us far away from love between equals, philia, to the bossy older sister love of storage. Targets driven by a vicious internal voice that demands we sacrifice everything to save the world. Health workers often have superegos like tanks, making us vulnerable to overwork, building crescendos of resentment and burnout. The superego is that internal bully that propels us towards yet another categorical imperative when our precious hearts are screaming out 'mate, it is your spiritual duty to stay on the sofa eating crisps'.

Some of the most difficult learning experiences used in some psychodynamic clinical training programmes are experiential groups, where small groups of students spend an hour a week 'experiencing the group'. I spent a year of my life having weekly experiential group meetings with eight other people. Most of them I liked outside of the room, but during these sessions I felt persecuted and convinced that one member actively wanted to kill me. The experiences are so intense because the aim is to allow yourself to feel the full extent of your feelings about the dynamics in the room, something we are continually trying to deny and manage. I am not saying that anyone in the group did actually want to kill me, but we were brave enough to allow ourselves to feel the hate and violence that other people evoke in us as preparation for the onslaught of unconscious fantasies and communications that get projected in the consulting room.

During this period I learned an enormous amount about myself, most of it unattractive and disturbing to my carefully manicured sense of who I am. Subsequently I never now start a sentence with the words 'I'm the kind of person who . . .'. In my mind I am someone who has a particular role and position in my relationships, influenced heavily and unconsciously by growing up in a small rural community and being a twin. In groups, however, we learn that the roles can change with different people and within groups at different points in our lives. During crises certain roles are emphasised and others denied – the hero, depressed, angry, resistant to change, the stoic. Just as everyone with a past life was Cleopatra or Anthony, we like to think that we are all heroes. Although I actively hated the experience, it proved to be a profound learning experience to find out that we are all human beings subject to the dynamics, anxieties and insecurities of being in groups.

Experiences in groups also show us that the people who have a role in your survival at work are not always the people you love or are intimately tied to. This is clear if you look at union membership. Joining a union when your job is at risk is not a complex decision; it is a necessity that most working people understand. Collective power and legal expertise are two very important reasons for joining, but this does not mean you actually love your representative or start branch meetings with a group hug. Many reps (I say this as someone who has worked for and within trade unions for most of my adult life) are not always all that likeable. Some actually dislike their own membership, much like teachers who hate children and librarians who do not read books – a perversion that exists in most professions. But for many of us their presence at a disciplinary is the difference between survival or not.

Our relationships with the people we work with, often hilarious and lovely, can also be fractious. What is important here is that we understand emotionally that collectivising is central to our survival because it offers us a chance to grow and adapt in a way we cannot do alone and a profound sense of place and support in the process. In today's workplace that is priceless. It does mean accepting the uncomfortable, irritating and often ridiculous behaviours and views of other people. When you have got over that, you might find that some of them are actually quite nice.

Whatever your workplace politics, love and its absence is always involved. Despite the frustrations, a politics of love is worth it because it is in the mix between us that the revolution happens. The rest is just being able to live with yourself.

Reading

Bacon N (2010) *The State of Happiness: Can Public Policy Shape People's Wellbeing and Resilience.* London: The Young Foundation.

Britton R (2015) *Between Mind and Brain: Models of the Mind.* London: Karnac.

Cederstrom C & Spicer A (2015) *The Wellness Syndrome.* London: Polity Press.

Davids MF (2011) *Internal Racism: A Psychoanalytic Approach to Race and Difference.* London: Palgrave Macmillan.

Davies W (2015) *The Happiness Industry: How the Government and Big Business Sold Us Well-Being.* London: Verso.

Hammond P & Bousefield A (2011) *Shoot the Messenger: How NHS Whistleblowers Are Silenced and Sacked.* London: Private Eye Special Report.

Hoggett P (1992) *Partisans in an Uncertain World: The Psychoanalysis of Engagement.* London: Free Association Books.

Holt K & Kline R (2012) Whistle while you work – if you dare. *Health Service Journal* 25 October. 122(6326):22–23.

King Eden B & Dawson J (2011) Why organizational and community diversity matter: The emergence of incivility and organizational performance. *Academy of Management Journal* 54:1103–1118.

Kline R (2014) *The "Snowy White Peaks" of the NHS: A Survey of Discrimination in Governance and Leadership and the Potential Impact on Patient Care in London and England.* London: Middlesex University Press.

Layard R (2005) *Happiness: Lessons from a New Science.* London: Penguin Books.

NHS Employers (2012) *Speaking Up.* London: The Stationery Office.

Sedgwick P (1982) *Psycho Politics.* London: Pluto Press.

Seligman ME (1990) *Learned Optimism: How to Change Your Mind and Your Life.* New York: Random House.

Turquet P (1975) Threats to identity in the large group: A study in the phenomenology of the individual's experiences of changing membership status in a large group. In: Kreeger L (ed) *The Large Group: Therapy and Dynamics.* London: Maresfield Library.

Wachter Robert M (2008) *Understanding Patient Safety.* New York: McGraw-Hill.

Williams Mark G, West M, Bastin L, Teasdale J, Segal Z & Kabat-Zinn J (2007) *Mindful Way through Depression: Freeing Yourself from Chronic Unhappiness.* New York: Guildford Press.

6 Groups and gangs

"We're working in a culture of bullying and fear, and most people just shut up. Because people are working in silos they're not used to talking to each other. They're certainly not used to disagreeing with each other. Particularly when it comes to the huge conflict between the clinicians and the finances in the NHS."

Surviving work conversation: groups and gangs

ANGELA: I'm absolutely sure that working in a gang in a hospital or wherever has got something to do with being acceptable to the dominant culture. So if there is a clique in there who have the power you have to choose – am I going to be part of that gang that has the power or not? I know people who have watched bullying and have felt too ashamed and scared about their own job to whistleblow. The wish to be part of something – a tribe, a group or a profession – we know is a huge pull. The shame of watching something and not doing something – either you're letting down the gang, or yourself, or your colleague, either way you're lost.

ELSIE: I think you have to be able to recognise that something is seriously wrong and it's actually going to damage me if I don't do something about it. I also think you need somebody on your side – somebody to support you and just guard your space, to be an ear and to point you in the direction. I had to find people and things to help me help myself. To be honest, although I didn't want to hear it I was told twice to leave the organisation – twice! – leave before they push you out. Sometimes you have to leave. You also need to contain the situation so it doesn't affect the rest of your life – because it can actually destroy your family life, professional life, everything that is you. It can destroy you. So you have to find some way of dealing with the situation, putting it down and getting on with the rest of your life.

ANGELA: Catch it early before it's gone too far. So if you had an awareness of what counts as ethical behaviour and reasonable requests from management and sets of behaviour – if you can catch it early enough before it becomes damaging. You need a touchstone – a reflective group, a thoughtful individual – before you go mad. Once you've got to the point of bullying where you're in pieces you can't hear it so being able to take it to an ally to say, 'What's going on?' and to hear someone say, 'This is not on'. So that the moment it happens you're not isolated.

ELSIE: Just talking about gang culture, in my case I couldn't understand why people were looking on and not doing anything because it was very visible what was happening. Nobody did anything, except for this one person who actually saved me. Really, nobody said anything – it was as if they were complicit in what was going on.

ANGELA: And immobilised by the whole system. We shouldn't be – we see it around us, and what resilience we need to whistle blow as you did. I'm not excusing this – it made me think that I was in the wrong – they're in the right, look most of the people aren't saying anything so why am I making such a big fuss?

ELSIE: But would you then be a whole person? You see for me you need to resolve these things. I feel like I wouldn't be a whole person just standing by. I feel a bit uncomfortable now because now I meet my bully at work – and it's a hello and a hug and we've resolved it and put it down. Well, I have.

ANGELA: You've done the work. After years of thinking about this and understanding and reading and PhDs you're understanding bullying. And it's hard, it's hard to be always conscious and thoughtful and ethical. Not everybody can do it.

To hear the full conversation with Angela Eden and Elsie Gayle go to www.survivingworkinhealth.org.

Groups and gangs

If you ask most people if they actually like groups they will say no, precisely because they can make us feel afraid and persecuted. For the more paranoid amongst us, going to a team meeting or a Christmas party can provoke the same physical reaction as the prospect of playing naked outdoor netball on a February afternoon with everyone who has ever bullied you.

The experience of being in groups raises powerful feelings in us, often taking us back to earlier experiences of being in the family or at school, leaving us feeling infantilised and overwhelmed at the prospect that nothing ever changes. When things are working well, being in a group, like being at work, brings with it feelings of belonging and a concern for other people. Being with other people brings with it enormous benefits including social capital, learning and collective problem solving. Problems at work are much easier to handle successfully if we work in functioning teams, but the reality is that all groups go through periods when they do not function well and when gang-like states can become embedded.

Groups can stop functioning for many reasons, including the impact of restructuring, economic problems and poor management. Common survival strategies include withdrawing from colleagues or striking up alliances with people who offer us protection. When groups become dysfunctional we can think about them becoming gangs, characterised by a denial of reality and a shift in focus away from the primary task of work (producing stuff, caring for people) towards self preservation. The point at which the patient's needs do not matter.

Dysfunctional groups are difficult to change in a climate of recession, which many of us are determined not to acknowledge, preferring the security of operating within a closed system. Change, particularly enforced change, does something weird to people because it requires an adaptive response which can often trigger responses that are even more entrenched in toxic roles and patterns.

Another reason why groups can make us feel anxious is that they are difficult to understand, making us feel confused and disoriented. Business school libraries are filled with books on organisational behaviour and occupational psychology – to try to help people understand the dynamics at play. The hope is that by building a solid understanding, individuals and organisations can function in more productive and healthy ways, particularly important in healthcare where there is little place for fantasy and fiction.

Gangs exhibit three main characteristics. First, gangs present a uniform front, with a shared and powerful identity. Gang members do not try to be individuals or single themselves out. Second, gangs create their own realities and rules as a way of protecting themselves from the outside world and which members do not question. Ever. Third, gangs project unacceptable feelings and characteristics onto the outside world, particularly other gangs or people who are perceived to be weak in some way.

Gangs create a fantasy world where you can be part of a powerful group of cool kids who take on the bad guys and push around the little people. Gangs deny differences – particularly between members – and as a result nobody gets to question the rules or dabble in free expression. Gangs can exist everywhere there are groups of people, starting way back in those glorious days of the playground. This paranoid regime involves securing a position in the workplace aristocracy, where being top dog no longer means being a team player; rather, it is about how to keep a critical mass below you on the evolutionary scale. What this leaves us with is a tight group that functions on a really basic level, denying any differences within the group and picking fights with groups and scapegoating individuals on the outside.

Group dynamics are dominated by our attempts to avoid anxiety. The rage at our own vulnerability at work can bring out what Bion calls our internal 'chaos monster' – the panic we feel when everything is not clear-cut and we have to deal with the troublesome, complex stuff of working with people who do not share our DNA.

Anxiety in groups can do bad stuff to people – connections and links are broken, and the world gets split into good and bad. Many of us hide behind our ideological or professional defences and retreat into a religiosity and righteousness. This is a state of mind where beliefs become facts and being right turns into being self-righteous.

In a way the issue of gang formation is a problem with no solution. In situations of crisis the shift from group to gang is very likely to happen. This uncomfortable fact is precisely why I am a big fan of a psychodynamic model of working with groups because it does not try to solve the facts of life; rather, it tries to help us deal with them.

To admit that gang formation is an inevitable part of working life is not the politics of defeat; rather, it is the belief that life is about making the best of a bad lot and that by understanding group dynamics – what they are, how they get established and how to keep gangs in their place – we can contain them. I regret that this process is not a ride for the faint-hearted because there is no psychic Ketamine to escape looking at some grim realities. However, it is a process that can ultimately build your capacities to survive work for the long-term by offering an alternative to the dominant short-term defences.

In the likely event that the group you work with goes through a period of functioning like a gang, the proposal of this chapter is that at some point the tactic of retreat will become counterproductive. That, instead, building our capacity to understand and manage group dynamics offers us a longer-term way to deal with the inevitable problems involved in working with people who are not exactly the same as us.

The B word

Bullying is psychic paint stripper, effortlessly removing shiny surfaces and protective shields. It is a powerful chemical which can strip away our sense of ourselves and our place in the world. Bullying at work is painful in part because it pretty much always involves a crowd – the witnesses, the didn't-see-nothings, the cheerleaders and the bullies themselves – turning departments into ghettos and teams into gangs.

Despite everything we know about the necessity of teamwork in health and social care, where bullying exists we generally do not challenge it. Getting a perspective on bullying is difficult because it requires facing up to some hard facts of life. It is tempting to get all legal about bullying, and indeed bullying is bad, but you cannot ban it. I don't wish to rain on your parade of human loveliness, but bullying is an ordinary part of life which gets delusions of grandeur during a crisis. In a recession we live on the edges, rubbing along, bumping into each other and then sometimes we literally collide.

Here is the bullying problem. Human beings + recession + power differences = fear = paranoia + splitting = bullying.

Bullying is not an exact science, it is something like 'the repetitive, intentional hurting of one person or group by another person or group, where the relationship involves an imbalance of power' (The Anti-bullying Alliance) – underlining the structural inequalities behind bullying.

Bullying raises profoundly disorienting questions about our own sanity and culpability. Often the victim of bullying experiences a dumbing down, questioning basic facts about what just happened and who did it. This confusion is a way of denying the problem. If I cannot work out what bullying is then maybe it did not happen. Silly me, must grow a pair before the next staff away day.

Playing stupid is a perfectly normal way to protect ourselves from bullying but is hardly becoming of a professional, so I often use a definition used in schools from the Anti-Bullying Alliance website: 'Bullying is saying or doing something horrible to someone else, more than once. The person doing the bullying knows their actions are upsetting'. The simplicity of that statement makes me want to cry. Someone repeatedly, knowingly making me feel horrible. Have a little cry if you would like to.

At the risk of pointing out the really obvious, here are some examples of what bullying behaviours look like in work:

- Humiliation in front of others
- Deliberately undervaluing someone's work
- Demotion – real or implied

- Putting people into solitary confinement and excluding them from contributing to work
- Threats of disciplinary action for small or unsubstantiated incidents
- Refusal to discipline other staff for bullying behaviours
- Not explaining or giving training for new responsibilities
- Changing job description without consultation
- Refusal to talk directly or confirm in writing any complaints about work
- Aggressive behaviour
- Ridiculing; sarcasm; use of offensive names, jokes and language; spreading gossip
- Holding meetings the purpose of which is not clear and with short notice
- Refusal to minute meetings or allow representation at meetings
- Contacting employees at home or on holiday or sick leave with 'urgent' work
- Coercion into doing work that disregards rights and job descriptions

Getting a perspective on bullying is profoundly difficult because it requires facing up to some hard facts about human life. People hurt each other in an attempt to rid themselves of their own vulnerability, a paranoid attempt to split the world into powerful people and vulnerable ones.

Psychoanalytic ideas are profoundly useful in helping us understand how bullying has become established in a non-judgemental way – defining it as a psychological and social defence against our own feelings of vulnerability, anxiety and aggression. Under this model bullying is understood as an attempt to project our own vulnerability and fear onto other people, something that under the right (or wrong) circumstances we are all capable of doing.

With health workers, I often use an activity of designing a Bullying Campaign as a way of helping people see this dynamic. Each small group is asked to design a campaign with logos, strategic aims, policies, targets and tactics to establish a culture of bullying in their workplace. If we are feeling flush we make campaign T-shirts and badges. Most people are shocked to find they have a surprisingly mature understanding of gang warfare.

A common process in healthcare is where we project unacceptable or 'bad' qualities onto a group on the basis of their ethnic background. Despite the blinding evidence, very few of us talk openly about the reality that the NHS is, in fact, institutionally racist, with 25% of BAME staff consistently reporting they are discriminated against at work.

But once the discrimination data comes out we are still left with the enormous difficulties NHS staff are going to have in trying to tackle racism at work. Bluntly, racism is underpinned by a hatred for other people and rage at being on the receiving end of it. The data does not express the deep and difficult emotions that are inherent in experiences of discrimination and those involved in trying to stop it.

Just think about that for a second and imagine the chances of someone working in the NHS actually not knowing on some level that he or she works in a gang culture.

This predictable, assured and relatively secure psychic reality comes at the expense of living in the real world and fundamentally denies the possibility of positive change. This organisation acts as a paralysing force, making it hard to break out of essentially destructive and anti-life states of mind. I am not saying it's your fault that you might work in Gangland, rather that if we want to get out of it we have to face up to both the external and internal factors that got us there.

The internal bully

The hardest part of knowing that we are all involved in bullying at work is the realisation that there is some aspect of us that can dislike the people we work with.

When we encounter differences in others, particularly if we do not like them or are working in a workplace in conflict, the psychological process can go as follows:

- One of our beliefs, values or practices are challenged
- We become offended
- We get angry
- We become hateful towards the people around us
- We then experience a paranoid guilt that the other person is going to retaliate
- We get defensive and hostile

In most cases, our egos find it very hard to handle this decline into primitive feelings, so we deal with feelings of hatred often by withdrawing from other people. This dilutes the strength of our ugly feelings but also allows us to keep our views unchallenged and our superiority intact. In workplaces where bullying is accepted, we easily get sucked into a passivity, colluding with a psychic caste system that says the world is simply made up of weak people and strong people.

One much discussed idea in psychodynamic writing is that of the 'internal racist' developed by the psychoanalyst Fakhry Davids – that we all have an internal drive to hate difference in others, a feeling that is provoked under stress and situations of scarce resources.

An important dimension to bullying is what happens in the mind of the victim when the bully launches his or her attack. One of the reasons why bullies get under our skin is because they enlist our internal bullies: the voices inside our heads that actually agree with the external bullies. Bullies find people who believe they are destined to live with the other underdogs, believing in the bully's birth right to power. They do this because it takes us longer to work out that bullies become powerful because we give them that power.

This is particularly the case with toxic coping strategies like drinking and drugs where tackling them, particularly hard in the case of addiction, means standing up to this internal voice that bullies us into thinking we cannot cope without them. This is sometimes difficult to do because these voices can be powerful inhibitors of our self-confidence that we are good enough without these toxic props.

I promise you that I am wincing as I write this because it feels like I am punching puppies, but there is no way we can continue to tip toe around this. If we think that being a victim of bullying is just what happens to us underdogs, then we accept it rather than facing up to something that is in our hands.

This collusion between internal and external bullies means that dealing with bullying requires something of a psychic revolution. No, I am not going to get all Marxist on you, but I believe, as in any social movement, that changing workplace cultures requires raising our consciousnesses about reality and our belief in a world where there are haves and have-nots, bullies and victims, and never the twain shall meet. The reality is that they are meeting all the time internally and we cannot even get off the starting blocks of feeling good about ourselves if we do not face up to it.

Alternatively we can project the hell out of there by splitting and taking the road to righteousness. On this highway we divide the world into good people and bad people, taking retribution on the external bullies with eye-watering ferocity. This is a dump and run strategy that leaves us feeling guilty and weirdly unsure that we got it right. It is a destabilising position because deep down we lose our sense of what is right and what is wrong and the whole world of real life that is somewhere in between.

This internal bully can get even more powerful when we are having problems in life, such as being overwhelmed at work. For any of us who have been close to burnout, it is often not the fact that an employer undervalues our work but rather that not reaching the target triggers a tourette of internal criticism and reflections on how useless we are.

Getting out of the playground

Tackling gangs is actually a moral crusade for all of us because it is with great regret that I have to inform you that under stress anyone can move from that nice bloke in Accident and Emergency (A&E) to a leading role in *Breaking Bad*. This workplace reality presents us with a massive dilemma – how to stay connected to the people around us when everything in us wants to run screaming for the hills?

Although defences against gangs and bullying are important, long-term retreating from other people has consequences. John Steiner's book *Psychic Retreats* beautifully explores the defensive formation of mental bunkers that both protect us from perceived threats but also cut us off from reality and other people. Steiner describes this internal order as a mafia-like structure that re-establishes a sense of security by providing an internal organisation. Like the real mafia, it operates in an economy of threats (don't you *dare* question the order) and the offer of protection (if you accept the order then you will be safe).

Cutting to the chase, the simple answer is other people. This can be anyone, including friends, likeminded geeks, people who really want to do some work or that tried and tested option of joining a union. Trade unions are particularly good at dealing with bullies – they do not like them, and reps can be dogged in their devotion to shouting back on our behalf when we cannot summon up the strength to unlock the toilet door.

The reason for this is because when you are being bullied, you are on the receiving end of a projection which says that you are on the losing side. It plays on our vulnerabilities, cutting us off from our own and other peoples' humanity. The only way to tip the balance back is to rely, I would suggest heavily, on our own humanity and that of others. This requires making contact with other people and asking for their help.

Despite everything that seems wrong with telling someone who is being bullied to make contact with other people, joining a group can give us a profound sense of place and support. We need people on our side – people who are more on our own side than we are. Although running away might look like a ticket out of Gangland, without other people it is a visa to nowhere as there is always going to be a gang waiting at our next destination.

Psychoanalytic ideas promote a model of development which is about taking a view of the world that is not black and white. Growth involves a psychological process of moving away from a perspective where people like me are good and people who are not like me are bad towards a more depressive position that we are all a mixture of good and bad aspects. This more balanced perspective about the world allows us to reduce the very human default position to project our angry and negative emotions into other people. The argument is that by accepting we are all able to hate and love, we can then take some kind of ownership of the destructive emotions we all have to deal with in working life. It is on the basis of this humanistic view that we can try to bring about change and adaptation to the extent that gangs can be turned back into groups.

Sweat the small stuff

Having the dubious honour of working on bullying at work for some time, I am going to do something that I do not normally do, which is to give you a to-do list. I am doing this because even thinking about bullying can be disorienting, and sometimes having a short list can be very helpful. It is premised on a simple idea that tackling bullying requires sweating the small stuff.

Stage 1: find some higher ground

Being bullied feels like drowning, so you first need to get to safer ground. This involves getting out of bullying hot spots – anything from avoiding the smoking breaks or those after-work drinks that seem to end up with someone calling you fat and ugly – or going somewhere every day where you feel safe – from your best friend's sofa to train stations or allotments.

Stage 2: bullying book

Methodically write down the times, places and what happened every time you were bullied. Not everything is subjective; there are facts about bullying behaviours, so write them down. Keep the book at home and only ever open it when you are in a robust frame of mind and definitely not when you are drunk.

Stage 3: get a witness

It is essential that you tell someone what is going on. This can be someone who has witnessed the bullying or not, someone you like or not, but someone whom you trust to keep an eye on you. Telling someone does a number of things. It forces you out of your bunker and makes you admit what is happening.

Stage 4: phone a friend

Whether you are a victim of bullying or trying to help someone who is, there is a huge temptation to withdraw from other people. So this brings us kicking and screaming to a really obvious fact of life. Tackling bullying requires doing something totally counterintuitive – making contact with other people and asking for their help. As any clinician knows, the work of helping other people involves helping ourselves, which turns out to be the hardest part because it requires us to put aside our shame and ask another human being for help.

If you can regain your humanity by taking some small steps, you will then be in a better position to make the bigger decisions about how to tackle bullying at work. Acknowledging that bullying is an ordinary part of working life is not the end of the world, and it does not inevitably mean you have to walk away from your job. Ironically, the strength needed to face up to bullying involves accepting both power and vulnerability, all in the same love bundle that you are. It means that you are not just a victim, or not just a bully, but rather someone capable of both. This is what is sometimes called ego-strength, where you are neither good nor bad, but able to bear your human reality.

Working with people who are not exactly like us and who are in pain and distress means that being offended by others is an occupational hazard. The issue is not whether we will be offended, rather what we do with the offence. If we nurture it and leave it unchallenged it can turn to hatred and righteousness, fostering workplaces where some people are believed to be inherently better than others.

Reading

Baillien E and De Witte H (2009) Why is organizational change related to workplace bullying? Role conflict and job insecurity as mediators. *Economic and Industrial Democracy* 30(3):348–371.

Bion WR (1961) *Experiences in Groups and Other Papers.* London: Routledge.

Canham H (2002) Group and gang states of mind. *Journal of Child Psychotherapy* 28(2):113–127.

Einarsen S, Hoel H, Zapf D & Cooper C (Eds) (2011) *Bullying and Harassment in the Workplace: Developments in Theory, Research, and Practice.* London: Wiley-Blackwell.

Erlich (2006) Enemies within and without: Paranoia and regression in groups and organizations. In: Gould Laurence J, Stapley Lionel F and Stein M (Eds) *The Systems Psychodynamics of Organizations: Integrating the Group Relations Approach, Psychoanalytic, and Open Systems Perspectives.* London: Karnac, 115–131.

Field T (1996) *Bully in Sight: How to Predict, Resist, Challenge and Combat Workplace Bullying.* Wantage: Success Unlimited.

Menzies Lyth I (1989) *The Dynamics of the Social: Selected Essays II.* London: Free Association Books.

White S (2013) *An Introduction to the Psychodynamics of Workplace Bullying.* London: Karnac.

7 How to make friends and influence people

"*The healthy organisation is a myth. There isn't such a thing. All health organisations are going to get stuck because of the impact that the work is having on individuals. That means that its normal for the individual to be overwhelmed by feelings. And normal for the organisation to be overwhelmed by processes that interfere with thinking.*"

Surviving work conversation: how to make friends and influence people

ANTONIA: I really like the Buurtzorg case study – it's quite radical in that it unseats the notion of highly split up working and instead makes a single person responsible for all aspects of the care role with the cared-for person. Instead of the patient having lots of small visits of different people looking at different aspects of their care you have one highly skilled person, in this case a nurse, who is actually doing multiple tasks. The team element of it is great because it's the way they set up work which is thoughtful in the sense that, for example, they develop twelve people into a team and develop them to work in a specific geographical location. You've immediately got a bunch of people who are able to support each other in the community and then you've also got all of those practical problems – people being on holiday or timetable – then there's good interchange within the group. It makes lots of sense. When we're talking about efficiency savings we should be thinking about better service at less cost. Really impressive.

CLIVE: It brings responsibility back to the individual – not just responsibility but control as well because that individual is making clinical judgements and judgements about the whole person. The essential element is that the patient is allowed to influence their care and the individual carer can take responsibility for quality and moderate what is happening without reference to someone else. Where costs go up is when things get kicked up the hierarchy for someone else to judge, by some strange rationale that someone remote is in a better position to judge than the person on the ground. The carers get a lot more job satisfaction, which is directly linked to patient outcomes. Rather than being told from above what targets and procedures they have to do or limited by a silo mentality.

ANTONIA: There is a paradox in the NHS. That by splitting up the work task into smaller bits you get a lower quality service and lower productivity. The other side of that though is the importance of having people who have joined a profession – people who joined to be a nurse, a mental health specialist – people who have a deep knowledge of their area and now in order to provide whole person care, for example in cancer teams, then you want to have a bunch of specialists on a single task. You don't want silo mentality, but you do want people with the ability to bring together different expertise.

CLIVE: So that's where you need to build that into the work situation. People need collective and reflective time to look at the quality of the service. When we see the small but dreadful cases of the Bristol infirmary, there was no reflective time, no analysis of, 'How did we do?' You're right, it's a paradox, but it's also about creating a system where people recognise that there is a prescribed system for care but can also adapt it based on their own intelligence and will.

ANTONIA: There is the opportunity through Better Care Together to do some radical thinking in healthcare and cooperation between different agencies.

But often it's turned into programme management – lots of well-trained project managers and meetings reviewing Gantt charts and actions – we've now lost the philosophy of people finding out how to do things better together.

CLIVE: It's not just a method, it's a philosophy. It was against Taylorism and Fordism and it said, look, you take the responsibility back to the individuals. Forget the supervisors – they just cost you money and breathe down people's necks – just give people the opportunity to get things right the first time. It's a common cycle in the academic literature – plan-do-check-action – very simple. It's a continual cycle that, if you can, you get individuals, teams and managers to adopt.

To hear the full conversation with Antonia Maclean and Clive Morton go to www.survivingworkinhealth.org.

How to make friends and influence people

In the 'quasi' market system of the NHS – the largest employer in Europe with thousands of private, third-sector and NHS Trusts and Clinical Commissioning Groups within it – there is no one system of management in place. We have seen the growth of New Public Management (NPM) techniques in the NHS, driven strongly over the last ten years by attempts to cut welfare spending and drive public sector performance.

The point about management styles is not a chippy left-wing point about gaffers versus workers. Enormous efforts and funding have gone into the development of management into a super science. Since the 1980s, human resource management techniques have been imported from the US to support new ownership structures and economic policies. Many of these methods were used to develop individualistic forms of management – such as performance-related pay and appraisal systems – away from a model of collective management and an industrial relations system based on a tripartite dialogue between state, employer and trade unions or professional bodies.

Even if the targets that most NHS Trusts are working towards were feasible, there is still the inherent problem of running healthcare on the basis of nationally set targets, which rely on a bureaucratic system of measurements and inspections to manage them. This is a model of performance management which is at best blunt, at worst a punitive system of 'inspecting out' problems rather than trying to address them within clinical teams. It is a system that has very limited tolerance of the reality of human beings treating other human beings where information can be limited, solutions can be unclear and treatment has to be defined through a process of adaptation.

In response to this, the drive within NHS management is increasingly directed towards how to give staff the responsibility, scope and resources to produce good quality care that is 'built in' to the management system. This, in its simplest form, is all about finding ways to re-establish interdisciplinary and non-hierarchical teams that can promote group and organisational learning.

This is not to suggest that being a manager in the NHS is a comfortable place. A staggering 20% of senior management positions remain empty in the NHS – a figure that goes up to 37% in mental health. As demand for health and social care services go up in a context of recession and an ageing population, it appears that not everyone wants to take the lead in healthcare.

One cause is the brutality of the bullying culture that goes right to the top – reflected in highly publicised cases of senior management turned NHS whistleblowers. Leadership vacancies are in part due to the fear of 'double jeopardy' when clinicians take up senior management positions and find themselves with often conflicting organisational and clinical duties of care.

Research indicates that managers under pressure to deliver targets typically default to a command and control management style which is unresponsive to both patients and staff and is linked to workplace cultures where staff are reluctant to raise concerns and become disengaged and dysfunctional. The primary reason there is a problem with trying to manage people is that the management systems in place make this only a remote possibility. Because of the focus on productivity targets and financial cuts and the rigid systems of measurement put in place to manage them, there is not much room for actual people in the system.

It means that frontline mangers need to consider introducing different management practices as individuals – without putting a neon sign over their heads saying 'independent thought going on'. It may mean, for example, introducing reflective practices within your immediate teams and seeing what comes out of it. The more everyone talks the easier the really hard work of restructuring and negotiating will be.

This section is for the frazzled and dazzled people trying to manage teams. Although there are no magic solutions to the structural problems of managing healthcare, the proposal is that managers – whether clinical or not – should reorient away from targets towards teams using a tried and tested model of interdisciplinary and interorganisational team working.

This is a tradition of democratic leadership where teams are the primary unit of management and hold the collective responsibility for performance. This model was developed in the manufacturing sector in the 1980s using a Japanese model of team building – a 'support and stretch' as opposed to a 'control and constrain' culture which emphasises interdisciplinary and experiential learning and importantly is linked to high clinical results.

The limits of the system

In 2015 social care in the UK underwent a serious reality check when the Care Quality Commission (CQC)'s social care chief, Andrea Sutcliffe, claimed in the *Guardian* that a chronically underfunded system is 'turning good people into bad carers', with 150 complaints about elderly care raised every day. At the same time our attention turned to Buurtzorg, a Dutch social care company, that toured around the UK in the same year to promote a radical model for high quality social care at 65% of the going rate. It does this by getting rid of administrators and letting carers organise their own work.

Buurtzorg now employs over 7,000 frontline staff, representing 60% of Dutch community nurses, with just thirty managers on its books. The costs per hour are higher, but patients need 30%–40% less contact time every month. Nurses work in teams of ten, each serving a particular community and working reactively to patient needs. They work closely with local GPs and local services and see themselves as having a key social function identifying and building relationships within the community. Not only are patients happier, but so are staff, with 60% less staff absenteeism and 33% lower turnover. Never have 1980s nursing management techniques been so en vogue.

This model of care is in stark contrast to the UK where 160,000 social carers earn less than the minimum wage and social care job vacancies are higher than any other sector. Most of the people who currently work as carers are the real deal: women, middle aged, many of whom worked for the public sector and still remember what professional ethics and standards look like. Currently 50% of private providers come from the not-for-profit sector, many of which were set up during privatisation. Within the next decade most of these carers will retire, and with them goes our heritage of how to manage social care, old school.

A pragmatic attention to efficiency and cost savings through technology and clinical practice is attractive, but the Dutch model comes from a very different institutional setting. Comparative Employment Relations, sometimes called the Varieties of Capitalism model, offers us a theoretical framework for understanding how and why work is organised differently in different countries. Within this perspective, the UK and Netherlands, despite both being capitalist systems, are profoundly different in their approach to providing care. Two institutional factors really stand out.

The first is that Dutch institutions are framed within a political culture of social democracy and based on strong egalitarian principles. The Dutch and Nordic countries have a shared emphasis on equality, reflected in the lack of pay differentials and a dominant workplace culture of flat leadership. To maintain this equality, the Netherlands has one of the strongest welfare systems in the world.

The second institutional factor relates to employment relations. Although wages by UK standards are moderate, Dutch workers are compensated by a generous 'social wage' including high unemployment benefits, labour protections and social security benefits. It means that although senior executives are not necessarily mega-rich, only 3% of Swedish workers are classified as low wage as opposed to 22% in the UK.

These differences are seen most clearly if we look at flexible work in health and social care sectors. Unlike the UK's often brutal neo-liberal model of high flexibility and insecurity, the Dutch model specifically tries to balance the demand for flexible working with the security needed by flexible workers – in the EU called 'flexicurity'.

The Dutch system protects carers from falling into in-work poverty and de-skilling by having higher protections and investment in skills development. This security includes a higher percentage of flexible workers who are represented by Dutch trade unions, including new unions designed specifically for self-employed workers.

With a £22 billion efficiency challenge and 'restructuring fatigue' within UK health and social care, it's tempting to go for a technical solution to a political problem by cutting the 48% of non-clinical staff in the NHS. There's nothing wrong with importing new management ideas – we did it in the 1980s with Japanese production methods – but to do this successfully we have to understand the institutional systems within which they can work.

Cutting bureaucracy is only one part of the socio-political equation because the Buurtzorg model is one of workplace autonomy and democratic leadership where decision making and setting targets are decentralised to clinical teams. The UK and Netherlands' profoundly different institutional settings – not least the shameful fact that the UK is the most unequal society in Europe – means that to do this successfully would require an enormous shift in both the UK's employment relations system and workplace cultures. Although not impossible, we have to face the difficult issue of public sector management in the UK head on.

Performance management in the NHS

Given that the NHS is the largest employer in Europe, there is no one model of management in place. New Public Management techniques have been adopted to drive performance and improve 'efficiencies'. In most healthcare settings management involves both clinical and organisational teams – sometimes in the same person but increasingly with a clear divide between the two.

The fate of the manager in the NHS is fickle. There have been periods where NHS 'leaders' have been seriously developed and trained – with a recognition of the enormous range of skills required to balance the needs of different constituencies. UK business schools used to give a collective sigh of relief when their NHS contracts were renewed – with NHS management students the cream of the crop, smart mainly young women who bucked the Dragon's Den model of business school cultures.

In the management literature there is debate about what is happening to management in the NHS. The decline in the 'public sector ethos' seems inevitable within the administration of an increasingly privatised healthcare system. The emphasis of management shifted from human resources to contract management and measuring financial outcomes.

Maybe unsurprisingly, research of clinical groups indicates that professional codes and commitment to the NHS remain strong. The vast majority of clinicians continue to describe their employer as the NHS when in fact they work for a contractor or third party. This different orientation between clinicians and service managers might explain the regular miscommunication between these two levels of management as they often see the nature of what they are managing in different ways.

The research also indicates that there has been a growth in a hierarchical 'command and control' system of management from national to local levels in the NHS. It is common that managers tasked with delivering non-negotiable targets will default to a command and control style – do this now exclamation mark. Managers easily become insensitive and defensive to the problems of matching these targets to patient care and 'thick skinned' to the distress within teams that this causes.

The suggestion is not that managers are bad people – far from it – rather that as human beings we easily slip into bad habits under the wrong conditions. Command and control management is easy and is often slipped in through small mistakes and omissions such as:

- Not making sure staff were adequately trained when new equipment was installed
- Changing conditions of work without consultation or agreement
- Questioning staff 'attitudes' and 'negative thinking'
- Constantly disputing leave and sickness absence
- Cancelling team meetings or filling them up with forms and procedures
- Never letting people say what they actually think

The system actively encourages managers to reduce quality of care – such as prioritising short-term treatments for long-term conditions and sending people home before they are actually better. This damages the relationships within teams and puts clinicians into direct conflict with their own professional codes and duties of care. Most managers will be blissfully unaware of the minutiae of clinical practice and codes, instead seeing a clinician refusing to discharge a patient as someone who just will not do what he or she is told.

Additionally, it is now considered acceptable to expect clinical staff to spend increasing time and resources measuring and reporting outcomes against targets. There are a number of problems with this algorithmic system. First, it's taken about fifteen years to set up electronic systems of measurement that actually work. All of a sudden systems need upgrading, and it really does feel like we are back in the 1980s when a twelve-year-old turns up to install new software and middle-aged staff consider early retirement because they are feeling defunct. Even when we have tablets and PCs, because of the time it takes to fill in this data (in many cases it has to be filled in within twenty-four hours), people do the paperwork at home. Hardly a model for healthy working.

More importantly, this system of measurement and reporting has a profound effect on how people are managed. The job of caring gets carved up, with part-care tasks such as medication or assessments separate from actual treatment. This Taylorist version of healthcare reduces the job that needs doing to part-processes rather than clinical care that treats the whole person. It means that managers and clinicians are often speaking completely different languages for care.

Service managers often come from other sectors or have limited experience of clinical settings. Over the last ten years the training offered to managers has become shorter and more focussed on fighting fires and project management than the realities of managing services in crisis. If we take mental health services, a major cause of concern for clinicians is the lack of management knowledge about what they do and the conditions required for delivering good services. From protecting private consulting rooms to having long-term planning of services, the capacity of the manager to really understand the nature of the clinical work is key. It means that a willingness of managers to adapt to their specific clinical teams rather than use a generic model of project management is a requirement. On this point many clinicians struggle to build an alliance with service managers who are not receptive, and a cold war can set in – where management contact is limited to feedback forms and emails sent at four on a Friday afternoon.

The reality for all frontline managers is that nothing gets done without cooperation between clinical and non-clinical services. Getting interdisciplinary teams to work together is the meat of healthcare management – inherently complex and for some of us really interesting. Frontline managers of course vary in their natural styles and abilities, but given the nature of the emotional work in healthcare one of the qualities that is highly effective with teams is a level of emotional 'intelligence' and capacity to deal with the often deep feelings that come up in the work. To do this there has to be a level of authenticity in the way that managers manage – one which recognises the subjectivity of our experiences and the need for teams to influence how work is done. The margin for doing this is very tight in the NHS but not impossible.

From targets to teams

There is an inherent problem of running healthcare on the basis of nationally set targets, which rely on a bureaucratic system of measurements and inspections to manage them because it is essentially a punitive system of 'inspecting out' problems rather than trying to address them within clinical teams. It is a target orientation that has very limited tolerance of the reality of human beings treating other human beings where information can be limited, solutions can be unclear and treatment has to be defined through a process of adaptation.

A team-oriented structure, on the other hand, would give staff the responsibility, scope and resources to produce good quality care that is 'built in' to the management system. That is, the team's management of cases sets the targets and therefore the measurements, rather than the other way around.

The research indicates that for teams to function they need clear goals, supportive line management and good training. Maybe most important, teams require that members can raise concerns without fear of attack or victimisation and that their concerns will be taken seriously enough to be addressed collectively by the team. This model of teams, spearheaded by the writings of Alimo-Metcalfe, Gittel, Ghoshal and Nonaka and Takeuchi, is one where, unlike command and control management which blocks learning, teams are set up precisely to learn.

What we know from the research is that inclusive teams – which promote diversity, working across disciplines and democratic practices – are significantly better at capturing knowledge and promoting organisational learning. Where teams are inclusive they have a tendency to widen their pool of experience and knowledge and to encourage dialogue and the exchange of ideas. This allows for organisational learning, which can be linked to increased public sector productivity and patient safety.

Democratic leadership

All well and good, but how do managers create dialogic cultures in contexts where most people manage work by keeping their mouths shut and doing what they are told? At the policy level this inclusive model is a no-brainer that is gaining widespread support, but the difficulty remains in actually doing it.

This is in part because for people to participate at work they have to be allowed to speak their minds, make decisions about their work and challenge their own leadership without penalty. Within this tradition of what is sometimes called democratic leadership teams are the primary unit of management and hold the collective responsibility for performance. This model was developed in the manufacturing sector in the 1980s using a Japanese model of team building – quality circles and continual improvement being key aspects to it – now so integrated into UK management in other sectors we no longer use the term 'Japanese production methods'.

Democratic leadership prioritises practices of listening, observing, auditing, self-awareness, social-awareness and emotional management techniques. It requires a demanding regime of democratic practice and emotional intelligence from frontline managers and a radical departure from the current management culture. The aim is to create a workplace where I can say what is on my mind and you can bear to listen to me.

The 'group relations' tradition is an attempt to use psychoanalytic insights and practices to understand groups and build cooperation within them. Based on the pioneering work of Bion, Miller, Trist, Jacques and Rice after the Second World War and contemporary thinkers such as Armstrong, Menzies Lythe and Obholzer, this tradition involves establishing processes that build understanding and cooperation within groups. If you read only one book, *The Unconscious at Work*, edited by Anton Obholzer and Isabel Menzies Lythe, is pretty much the best book I have ever read about managing groups in healthcare.

The keys to building functional teams here is creating a task-oriented focus and adaptability in the face of difficult realities. Both of these aims require that people are able to work reflectively and responsively, so within this model groups are self-organised. This is a model where the deep barriers to democratic practices are addressed through the understanding and development of group relations.

The proposal of this book is that the job of a manager is to create the conditions where the relationships needed to do this can be formed. It requires not just building the business case for patient services but also a profound reorientation towards team building. A model of human being management (HBM) over the current preference in health and social care for managerialism. This proposal emphasises the capacity of managers to listen and observe group dynamics, build dialogue within teams and create safe environments where people feel able to do that. We look at these in turn.

Observe and learn

Understanding group dynamics, and what is going on under the surface, is profoundly important in managing actual people. A specific method used within psychoanalytic practice and adult education is to carry out workplace observations and analyse the material of the observation in workplace supervision groups. Although now rarely used in healthcare training, this method of carrying out observations at work, which includes taking notes and preparing a report for the supervision group whose aim is to analyse and understand what has been observed, is a powerful and useful way to spend time looking at what is going on. This practice of workplace observations and supervisions is still used in psychotherapeutic training in part because it provides a powerful opportunity to understand complex and unconscious dynamics at work.

Taking the time to observe workplaces is crucial because of the reality that most of us are trying to hide problems rather than expose them. Nobody is ever going to come to your office to say, 'Hi, I'm systematically bullying my co-workers because I'm scared that you are going to fire me'. It means that as a manager you often have to work harder and put aside your busyness to find out what is not being spoken about at work. This does not have to be done in any scientific way, just regularly enough for you to learn how to observe well.

Here are some practical suggestions:

- Spend time every day observing how people relate to each other; your gut reaction and how you feel during these observations will give you a clue about what is going on under the surface
- Watch out for changes in atmosphere at work – for example where a previously cheerful team becomes silenced
- Using anonymous surveys such as wellbeing and stress can provide good indicators of problem areas
- Track how grievances and conflict are handled – for example whether people who have raised concerns in the past have been victimised or excluded
- Try to get an accurate picture of the team or organisation, including recent history – such as whether there has been a high turnover of staff or recent contracting out of services

In a climate where you are under massive pressure to solve problems, it might seem a distraction to just observe. But by observing we can understand problems more deeply, and with that comes the ammunition to tackle them in more effective ways. If you are responsible for problem solving you may as well solve the real problems rather than the sanitised versions that tend to come up in department meetings. What I know about human relationships at work can pretty much be condensed into two simple facts.

Actually talking to people

Actual fact 1: If you ask people what their reality is and listen to the answer, you will definitely learn something. Do it enough and you are facing the prospect of a profoundly loving and political act – to become the change you want to see in your workplace rather than just banging on about it.

Developing people at work means treating them like adults. Adult education takes as a given that we all have experience of the real world and that the easiest way to learn is to start with that. In workplaces learning takes place when people can talk to each other – a model which emphasises egalitarian, transparent and discursive approaches to defining and solving problems. The reason why these methods work is that they are ideally suited to stimulate solutions to workplace problems based on the collective experience within the team.

This process requires setting up 'communicative spaces' where people feel able to talk. In workplaces where people avoid staff meetings or someone always dominates the discussion it might mean finding other spaces to talk to people or being a bit firmer about how conversations are managed. People always work and talk more freely in small groups, so if a larger setting is not working find a small group space for about five or six people to open things up.

I can condense twenty-five years of working in education into one small technique which I use every day of my working life. Never start any meeting, conversation or event without first asking the people you are talking to what the issues are for them. It can be as simple as 'what shall we start with today?' or 'tell me what kind of day you're having' – anything to get the other person to set the agenda for dialogue. Sometimes this requires awkward silences as people summon up the enthusiasm to respond, but it's a silence worth holding, so try not to fill it for them. People are easily pleased with you asking a genuine question and even more pleased if you have the respect to listen to the answer. But much more importantly, if you start your conversation asking them what is important, your job as manager is then focussed on what matters to your staff.

Another positive effect of encouraging people to talk to you and to each other is that we are often surprised at how smart and funny the people we work with actually are. Most of us whizz around in a blur of busy and have forgotten how to be nice to each other and why that might feel nice. It is always in my experience surprisingly reassuring and humanising to hear what other people have to say, even on tricky issues like team working.

This is not rocket science. Talk to the people you work with.

Creating safe spaces

Actual fact 2: This exchange between people is best done in a containing safe space where you do not get asked to leave for having half-formed ideas or not being productive. A thought crèche, if you like, where ideas can be developed and nobody is expected to have all the answers right now.

Developmental research shows that having a sense of security is the foundation of learning. If we are absolutely stressed out we literally stop thinking. Our minds go blank, we forget things we know and we lose our confidence in being capable grownups.

One of the key jobs of a manager is to create some 'safe spaces' where people can speak honestly to the manger and to each other. Experience shows that these spaces need to be informal, confidential and minus the neon sign saying 'place where difficult stuff goes'. Save that for the toilets. In the past these might have included smoking rooms or canteens – now they are likely to be at training workshops, particularly when they are off site.

The key to a safe space is that it is secure – so it is a space that is inviting and consistent, not constantly being used as storage or a meeting room. It does not have to be an actual physical room – it can be a regular event like supervision or reflective groups – but a space which is protected by the team.

In working life there is still a containing function that we need from our managers. Containment is an idea used in psychotherapy where the therapist provides this protective environment for the patient. This is done through using a therapeutic framework (regular hours, spaces and way of working) and developing a relationship where people feel safe and trusting. The same principles apply to the management of safe spaces. I am not suggesting that managers get a couch and a pipe, rather that dialogue has to be managed in a containing way.

The containment that these spaces can offer often comes down to the capacity of the manager to keep a secure framework. This involves not just keeping the space safe from outside elements, but it also means making sure that the principles of fairness, confidentiality and respect are followed. If someone acts out in the space – shouting, putting people down – then you have to address this in the room and not leave it for another time. People are very sensitive to whether you are confident enough to contain the group dynamics, so you have to be brave and clear in doing that.

Building a space can take some time, but usually in healthcare people have some experience of supervision and the practices and principles behind it. Clinicians for sure will be familiar with your attempts to create reflective spaces so you are likely to meet less resistance than you imagine. Sometimes groups cannot take what you offer them at the time you offer it – but that is not a reason not to create and continue to offer spaces for your team. At some point, if the need is there, the demand will follow.

The democratic manager

For many of us working on the front line the word 'leadership' conjures up images of shiny people with absolute clarity and certainty – a world of magic wands and magic PowerPoints. Comforting as it is to look upon the current NHS leaders as a separate form of human life, the reality is that most of them are ordinary people who started out wanting to do something worthwhile. The problem is that something happens in the political playground to downgrade our humanity. Two occupational hazards exist.

First, the people who go into leadership positions are highly motivated to do so. One of the problems with this genuine desire to do something in public service is that this belief can, with surprising speed and ease, turn into a sadistic guilt-pumping sense that it is your duty to save the world. This is equally true for clinical and organisational leaders. Add to this a certain degree of the old superhero syndrome where despite the political casualties littering the corridors of power somehow you have got what it takes to turn round the NHS. Voila – delusions of political grandeur.

For the people working as frontline managers and team leaders, taking up leadership positions is a big task. The job is probably impossible, and the splits between clinical and service staff, senior leadership and those of us further down the food chain make it a pretty depressing prospect. In my experience most frontline managers feel pretty badly about themselves because they feel they are failing every day.

A second occupational hazard is that in this situation it is tempting to become a hard-core manager whose beliefs become facts. Certainty and clarity with tick boxes and wall charts try to compensate for the anxiety we are feeling at work.

This fundamentalist defence splits the world into rights and wrongs and computer-says-no. This is a rigid system of management that restricts unnecessarily the scope for clinicians to adapt treatment to the actual human patient who is in front of them. The attack on clinical autonomy is one explanation why midwives are the most bullied professional group in healthcare. In talking to midwives the explanation for this, apart from patients and most midwives being women, is that midwifery demands that the midwife is totally partisan in responding to the needs of the mother. All clinical decisions are based on what the mother and baby need, not hospital procedures. In a clinical or managerial hierarchy this often puts midwives into direct conflict with colleagues at what could safely be described as a critical healthcare moment.

In his books *Sex, Death and the Superego* (worth carrying around with you in order to secure a seat on public transport) and *Between Mind and Brain*, the psychoanalyst Ron Britton explores the leadership mind. He argues that a fundamentalist position is a reaction to the profound human experience of needing to manage our anxieties in groups. He writes that it is not what we believe but how we believe that determines whether we can work together. If our anxiety dominates, our need for certainty goes up, which makes it very hard to maintain a more human position of 'moderate scepticism' about what is the best way to work.

In those warm-bath days pre-2008 human resource (HR) managers talked a lot about employee engagement as the key to productivity and profits. The professional body for HR managers – the Chartered Institute for Personnel and Development (CIPD) – produces annual figures on absence rates in the UK. Since 2008 absence has gone down, testimony to the fact that fear can have an equally galvanising effect as talent management. The trouble with a workplace strategy of fear is that you have to keep it up. As soon as people stop feeling scared they get angry, and managers will struggle to find an effective procedure for that one.

In stark contrast democratic leadership prioritises practices of listening, observing, auditing, self-awareness, social awareness and emotional management. It is through this emotional capacity that leaders become effective at building teams that are both realistic and resilient rather than grandiose and unresponsive to patient needs.

One characteristic of democratic management, whether at senior or frontline level, is to show some emotion. This is not a call for tears in the boardroom or team hugs; rather it is the argument that delivering democracy at work requires managers to address the deep and often destructive emotions that we all carry in our jobs. From getting to the bottom of bullying to addressing racism in the NHS, working life requires emotional intelligence as well as bravery.

Emotional intelligence can be defined as the capacity for self-reflection and self-regulation, empathetic qualities which allow us to understand the situation of the people around us and social skills which allow people to hear and observe reality as it is. In the case of health and social care this inevitably involves experiences of trauma, pain, distress and – not wishing to burst any human resource management bubbles – death.

People respond well to authenticity and find that when their manager holds off from yet another PowerPoint and just listens to them, it really works.

How to make friends and influence people

Oh dear, yet again I am resorting to bullet points, but I want to be sure I was clear about what this model means for managing healthcare.

First, wake up: Nobody will ever come up to you and say, 'I've got a terrible habit of humiliating my team and making them want to give up and die. Yup, really enjoy it, feel like a king amongst men. Living. The. Dream'. So open your eyes and spend a few hours a week just observing your teams and making your own mind up about what is not being said in those Monday morning catch-ups.

Listen and learn: Always start every interaction asking people what is going on and actually listening to the answer. If you have to ask twice, just do it.

Feel stuff: Getting people to work under these conditions means you have to be able to make contact with your own and other people's emotions. It means that your capacity to bear the difficult feelings of loss, frustration and anger is paramount in bearing the reality that everyone who works for you has strong feelings about their work.

Create safe spaces: Most people do not raise their concerns at staff meetings because they are frightened of being penalised for speaking their mind. To talk openly we all need to feel we are in a safe space to do this – and it is the job of a manager to try to create new or existing spaces so that people can speak openly to each other. Methods for doing this often come from adult education and focus around action learning sets or workplace supervision groups. It means establishing some ground rules for conduct, including respect and confidentiality. A good model for medical practitioners is used by the Balint Group and the Schwartz Centre. Other potential safe spaces include continuing professional development (CPD) workshops or taking a lead in team meetings – the key is to create spaces where colleagues are able to safely discuss their work.

Build alliances: To do anything in management you have to get buy-in from the people you work with. If you are going to influence people you have to make friends with them first. You should always make contact with other teams, managers and people further up the food chain. Even if you do not like them you need to at least be on 'hi, how are you?' terms before you can go to them with a problem. This means having your tag lines and business cases ready so that when you bump into them in the lift you can pitch.

Become a pedant: The details of work matter, massively. It matters if you define appropriate and inappropriate workplace behaviours, that your policies on speaking up guarantee confidentiality, that you give great training for all workers about diversity and really clear guidance on raising concerns. If someone is a bully, you have to address it head on.

Don't be brilliant: The more you set yourself up as a hero at work the more likely you are to end up feeling like a failure. Admitting that you are not brilliant already sounds like failure, and although it is probably not a great interview strategy, psychologically speaking, to survive being a frontline manager you have to know at a very deep level that being human is enough. By that I mean that sometimes you will make mistakes, not feel well and not know everything. You are also hopefully likely to get old and wear less fashionable clothes. This is OK. You are still a valuable and competent human being just like the rest of us.

As managers we have to let go of our superpowers and learn to rely on our ordinary human powers of making friends and influencing people.

Reading

Alimo-Metcalfe B & Alban-Metcalfe J (2005) Leadership: Time for a new direction? *Leadership* 1(1):51–71.

Arnaud G (2012) The contribution of psychoanalysis to organization studies and management: An overview. *Organization Studies* 33(9):1121–1135.

Berwick D (1990) *Curing Health Care: New Strategies for Quality Improvement.* San Francisco: Jossey-Bass.

Burton J (2015) *Leading Good Care: The Task, Heart and Art of Managing Social Care.* London: Jessica Kingsley Publishers.

Gawande A (2014) *The Checklist Manifesto: How to Get Things Right.* London: Profile Books.

Ghoshal S & Bartlett CA (1995) Changing the role of top management: Beyond structure to processes. *Harvard Business Review* 73(1):86–96.

Gittell H (2009) *High Performance Healthcare: Using the Power of Relationships to Achieve Quality Efficiency and Resilience.* New York: McGraw-Hill.

Kings Fund (2012) *Leadership and Engagement for Improvement in the NHS: Together We Can.* London: Kings Fund.

Morton C (2003) *By the Skin of Our Teeth: Creating Sustainable Organisations through People.* London: Middlesex University Press.

Nonaka I & Takeuchi H (1995) *The Knowledge Creating Company: How Japanese Companies Create the Dynamic of Innovation.* Oxford: Oxford University Press.

Peters T & Waterman R (2015) *In Search of Excellence: Lessons from America's Best-Run Companies.* London: Profile Books.

Rustin M and Armstrong D (2012) What happened to democratic leadership? *Soundings* 50(13):59–71.

Wattis J & Curran S (2011) *Practical Management and Leadership for Doctors.* London: Radcliffe Publishing.

Western S (2013) *Leadership: A Critical Text.* Second Edition. London: Sage.

8 Making the best out of a bad lot

"You don't lose your temper, you find it."

Surviving work conversation: making the best out of a bad lot

GERRY: A new NHS chief executive asked to see me, and he said, 'You have a ferocious reputation'. I just said, 'That's good because you've got a management team who are all bullies. If you stop that then perhaps my reputation will soften'. With other trusts I was alright. As a union rep you have to adapt to the situation you're working in.

ELIZABETH: I think that's a hard thing to take on the chin that often in times of conflict you're asked to adopt an aggressive position and then when it comes to other issues you're expected to come from a Swiss girls' finishing school. You have to be able to box quite fast between different positions.

GERRY: You can get a group of members who are angry about bullying, and you have to have the confidence to do something. In many cases you have to adopt a lead and agitating role. Then there comes a time when your position switches when you're looking for resolution. So you're almost going from an agitator to a meditator.

ELIZABETH: I used to do mental health work with trade unionists, and we had some fruity debates about the politics of mental health. But actually the thing that really stuck – quite similar to health workers – that you're forced into a position where you have to express the emotions of people who can't do that at work. Anger is the big one because although there's a lot of anger around conflict, and nobody wants to lose their job. Trade unionists are put in a position where they have to be angry when their members can't. The trouble is how do you calm yourself enough to then negotiate and then not be a complete nightmare in your personal life. You can't be angry all the time.

GERRY: You don't lose your temper, you find it. One thing I always say to members who are having trouble with managers is, 'What would you like me to say to them that you can't say?' That's quite powerful for individuals that someone will go in for them and say what needs to be said.

ELIZABETH: For me the job of a mental health worker and a trade unionist aren't so different because the job is to help people to articulate the things they cannot say. You're taking a position on something that's not right at a time when other people are vulnerable and can't say it. Intellectually they may know it, but emotionally it may be impossible to say. That's also the privilege of working as a rep.

GERRY: One of my closest colleagues is a community mental health nurse, and we used to talk about the parallels in the job. I used to watch him and sometimes say gently, 'You're looking at this as a mental health nurse; there now needs to be, you know, a little bit of action'.

ELIZABETH: So now we're coming to the politics of therapy – it's not enough to understand it, you've got to do something about it! That's the Marxist in me coming out, it's all about praxis. It's about knowing the world and changing the world. And there's a big debate in health about where the emphasis needs to lie. Doesn't matter what your ideology is, though, what we know is that working in health is now very political. The winding down of welfare, inequality, poverty of wages.

GERRY: Yes, it's a time bomb. And much of this is about discrediting public sector workers to discredit public services so that it shifts to a different system. I hope people wake up to that.

ELIZABETH: The other thing that's being lost is the experience of saying what you think without somebody beating you up or shooting the messenger. At their best, unions used to offer a space where people were protected and could say what was happening at work. There's the hope with the revival of grassroots organising that we can talk about the future, but the problem for health workers is that many are precarious workers who are frightened and when they're part-time don't have time to go to union meetings.

GERRY: I was in a meeting the other week and the rep said, 'How are we going to deal with these changes?' and I said, 'We're going to go and talk to the people who it's going to affect'. That should be our default position. If trade unionists don't talk to workers then they're not doing their job. The policies should develop from the people at the workplace.

ELIZABETH: In trade union education we're very strict about this – you never start any meeting telling people what the issues are; you have the respect to ask 'What are the issues?' and listen to the answer. It's from that that we build a collective response. We build solidarity by showing respect enough to ask the question 'What do you think?'

To hear the full conversation with Gerry Looker and Elizabeth Cotton go to www.survivingworkinhealth.org.

A proposal for surviving work

Over the last two years Jeremy Hunt has done more to unify the health sector than over 100 years of trade union organising and Corbynmania combined.

Nothing offends the scientific mind more than lies disguised as facts. The government's attempts to spin reality – from the underfunding of the NHS and the real costs of constant reform to who benefits from the privatisation of the NHS to why junior doctors took strike action for the first time in their history – have really galvanised health workers. The junior doctors' dispute, hardly the apex of class war, over pay and working conditions has been the frontline for the battle of the NHS. This was followed closely by the cutting of funding for nurses' training at a time when nursing shortages are the key threat to services, and there will no doubt be a continuous redrawing of the battle lines ahead.

Over the last two years it has been felt that anyone working in health is slowly morphing into Che Guevara, for some of us minus the beard. This is because the situation in healthcare has become so obviously unfair to both staff and patients that we are all being forced to take a position. This is not ideological, it is about social justice. Easy to pretend this is a left/right split, but the reality is that from both patient and provider perspectives, something very unfair has been introduced into the system. Still, in our culture, there is nothing quite like an injustice to get people onto the streets for another national demonstration. Fairness really matters to us.

In fact there is so much political activity in the NHS that it has become a full-time occupation just keeping up with campaigns in healthcare. In 2015 this led to the establishment of Health Campaigns Together to help coordinate action between key players like Unite, Save the NHS, Keep our NHS Public, Patients First and the thousands of networks of both patients and clinicians that have bloomed over the last few years. Importantly, there are hundreds of thousands of seasoned organisers in the UK, many developed through trade union networks, who are uncharacteristically en vogue. Our skills from organising picket lines to representing people in disciplinaries are very much in demand.

As someone who regularly goes to campaign meetings and events, I am pretty divided about the experience of campaigning around the NHS. Last year I remember sitting in a Unite meeting on a Saturday with like-minded folk watching the utterly brilliant Clare Gerada, the previous head of the Royal College of GPs, speak about the junior doctors dispute and the political battle within the British Medical Association (BMA), and I felt really sad. Why so glum, comrade?

One of the reasons was her acknowledgement that we lost the last battle when the Health and Social Care Bill was passed, pretty much killing off the institutions of public health. The battles over the NHS teach us that when you lose a major legal challenge to protecting public services, you never get them back.

This massive defeat, according to the people who drove the opposition through the unions and professional bodies, happened because of the self-interest of the people involved and the fragmentation of the rest of us. We did not actually stick together when it mattered.

Many organisers who have been active in the battle for the NHS are of a certain age and filled with a mixture of both love and loathing for this new 'movement' that is forming around social issues such as health and precarious work, such as the Deliveroo and Uber disputes.

Part of this ambivalence is a result of the bitter experience of what it actually takes to protect jobs and public services. We know from experience how hard it is to maintain public support in the long term and to get sufficient gains to keep people in decent jobs. The more precarious the workers, the more likely they can be bought or threatened off the picket line. If they lose their jobs in the process, they provide a cautionary tale to anyone with a collective glint in their eye.

Surviving work always involves both attempting to improve working conditions and surviving the existing ones. It is, like trade unionism, a dual process. It means that the struggle to stay in work is as important as creating a decent working environment, hopefully both but not always at the same time. Most of us cannot actually afford to lose our jobs, and that is a reality that has to take central place in any organising campaign.

In the workplace, the reality is that sticking together means sticking with people whom you may not see as taking the same position as you but whom you need. At any point this can include close colleagues, your union branch and management. Particularly in a workplace context, it is not always obvious which sides people will take, even people we consider on the same side.

In healthcare, this includes frontline managers who, far from being a separate specie, are in fact likely to have the same concerns as the 'workers'. Increasingly the status and pay of team leaders and frontline managers are not significantly different from their teams, and the distinction in terms of precarity is blurred. It means that allies are not always distributed on one side of the management divide.

Even if you have a good union branch in your workplace, the job of organising people is not straightforward. Having spent the last six months interviewing mental health workers, I am fully aware that unions are a patchy lot. Some branches and reps are actively loved by their members, others are not. It is not unusual to have to remind your branch several times of the problems you need help with, and in some cases you have to organise your own mini-campaign just to get your voice heard. It always involves phoning people several times, reminding them that you need help and attending union meetings to make issues visible. There is a huge competition for what union reps focus on, as they are usually overwhelmed with case handling for individual members, and

particularly around issues of equality and discrimination, which are complex and time-consuming processes. In my own case I have at points been blacklisted from my own union for trying to raise issues of mental health at work, and when I needed help the most, I was sorely let down one day before a compulsory redundancy interview. I do not underestimate the problems people can encounter getting their union to offer them adequate support, but at no point have I ever considered not being a member. When you find one of the many good reps who can take on your case, it is the difference between coming out of a bad situation in one piece or not.

Even when you have a great branch, it is still essential to be active in working collectively with colleagues and other members. A union is not actually made up of general secretaries and regional offices – trade unions are made up of their membership. It is the capacity of this membership to collectivise in workplaces that defines whether trade unions win negotiations. Although size to some degree does matter, mobilisation matters more, and this is work that has to be done before crisis hits.

Having functioning relationships between frontline managers and frontline workers is absolutely key to securing better working conditions. Even when this is done informally, it always involves some kind of negotiation. In order to get things you have to convince the other side. As a result, probably the key job of changing workplace conditions involves influencing people – particularly line managers – who can deliver improvements at work. Increasingly, frontline managers cannot secure higher staffing levels or pay – the reality is that the pressure has to go right up the food chain to the senior level. If you have a relationship with management, where difficult conversations can be had, then there is a much higher chance of being able to enter into negotiations over the bigger stuff with senior management. Enlist them where you can.

It means that our campaigns to improve working life cannot always rely on a tribal split between them and us, gaffers and workers, winners and losers – rather the more likely scenario is that compromise is going to be needed. This can only be achieved if you can actually talk to each other.

In a negotiation being right is not enough. It involves an emotional job of work of remaining open to people on the opposite side of the table and to model the behaviours that we want from them such as respect, understanding and not blaming the individuals involved. These behaviours are crucial to setting a basis for negotiations because ultimately whatever has been agreed upon has to be implemented, and that is where people being able to work together comes in.

The methods of solidarity

Despite the emphasis on relationships and dialogue within our healthcare traditions there is very little evidence that we are capitalising on our capacities and building the future solidarities we are going to need to promote and protect decent jobs.

The proposal of this final chapter is that we call on three bearded blokes to build a strategy for surviving work in healthcare. Namely Freud, Marx and Freire, all in their different ways the daddies of how to build solidarity at work. From how to have intimate relationships with the people around us to how to collectively problem solve, we have no choice but to bring out the radical big guns.

From Marx we can take the central objective of praxis – the attempt to understand the world and change it. The process of understanding what is happening in healthcare is not a theoretical case of reading books. Although books are good, understanding involves the challenging stuff of developing a critical perspective on why healthcare is organised in the way it is and who benefits from it. This is a process of consciousness raising – pursuing the facts and forming opinions that do not appear on the front page of the *Evening Standard*.

From Freud and Freire we can take the methods of relationality – how to collectivise and form relationships with the people around us. Emancipatory education, developed by the Brazilian pedagogue Paulo Freire, is based on the belief that the principal aim of learning is to establish ourselves as subjects with the capacity to define our own experiences, problems and desires and, subsequently, our capacity to act on the world. These models of education and psychoanalytic psychotherapy both emphasise the aims of emancipation and building relationality between people. They share a focus on understanding internal and external realities, using dynamic and dialogic processes in small groups and providing a containing framework where this important developmental work can take place. They are parallel developmental processes that share the principles and practices of how to work in groups.

Contentiously, both Freud and Freire recognise the uncomfortable fact that to overcome the external factors that inhibit decent working conditions we have to address the internal psychological factors too – the 'psychic oppressors', the internal voice that says people are rubbish and you cannot rely on anyone at work to help you stand up for yourself. Both psychoanalysis and emancipatory education recognise that living a full life is both a political and personal battle to overthrow the 'oppressors' that exist inside and outside our minds. A more palatable way of thinking about this is that development always involves a process of emancipation and building our sense of our capacities to make good decisions and the agency to determine how we work best.

I have spent most of my working life as an educator using these methods in workplace settings – from Thai activists in the industrial zones of Bangkok to the glorious Nepalese women working in German pharmaceuticals factories. This work over time re-oriented my entire relationship with the outside world and my internal one. I moved from left-wing religiosity – where I had the answer, comrade – to a sense of development as a collective process which I could not do alone. Within this model of adult education dialogue, genuinely practiced, is the basis for understanding ourselves and the world we live in and finding a way to muddle through.

You do not need to be a psychoanalyst or a liberation theologist to use the ideas and traditions these three bearded blokes created. The proposal is that the revival of these techniques and strategies that have a proven track record for diverse and precarious workers right across the world is worth a shot. Added to which we already have a structured system of workplace educators in the UK – through trade unions and the Workers Education Association. It is true that the emancipatory aims of trade union education took a total beating over the last twenty years, but the facts remain that we have thousands of skilled educator activists in this country. No need to reinvent the wheel, people, just find them and invite them to show you how to do it.

Under pressure not to mention Marx in the promotional literature for Surviving Work, I describe this model of emancipatory learning as the LAUGH framework. It's a bit slippery of me but necessary in these marketised times. This rephrasing of traditional methods can be re-described as:

Stage 1: Starting where you are by Listening and Assessing what is going on at work and taking a position on that

Stage 2: Understanding your environment and identifying resources you individually and collectively have

Stage 3: Getting help from the people around you and working out how to have better relationships at work

Despite the strangely excluding and sectarian ways of many activist networks, these methods are actually available to all of us to use. Ideological posturing, like beards, are not compulsory, and I find that after the first ten-minute monologue about neo-liberalism things generally calm down and you can have a genuine conversation with most people motivated to improve healthcare. Activism, at its very best, is just knowing how to form relationships with people that are strong enough to collectively respond to what is going wrong at work. I guarantee that you do not need to go on a correspondence course on Marxist dialectics or spend a decade in psychoanalysis to do this. It is as simple as talking to each other.

This drive to collectivise, although beaten up in the toilets of the NHS, is inherent in us, and the vast majority of health workers are naturally really good at it. For us it involves going back to our clinical roots. To start realistically, to talk and to stand up to the internal and external voices that say we cannot bring about positive change. To contain the anxieties that are flooding our consulting rooms and take some time to think about how we work. I am always humbled by the care and concern healthcare workers show to their patients. We now need to see that how we treat each other is a matter of equal ethical and professional concern.

Having worked in trade unions for much of my working life, there is not one romantic bone left in my body about unions as organisations. Regardless of how many committed and exceptional people work within them, they struggle like any organisation to keep it together. Most union reps are overwhelmed with case loads, and there is a high vulnerability of lay reps and activists to burnout as a result. Unsurprisingly, trade unions can be highly defensive organisations, which can make it difficult to become involved in their activities.

However, if the entire history of wage bargaining is anything to go by, without unions there will be no collective bargaining. Whether it is over living wages or agency labour, none of us have the capacity to secure our rights on our own. We need to freely associate to do anything of any significance. It is a no-brainer if you work in healthcare: just join a union.

One way to approach trying to build your relationships with colleagues is to use a strategic campaigning framework or techniques. What follows is a basic outline of what this might look like in healthcare settings – either with or without a union, whether a clinical team or just your immediate colleagues, this is a tried and tested framework that actually works.

Find out what people need

Probably the starting point for any organiser is to have the politeness to ask people what they think the problems are and what they think could be done to deal with them. Most people will not put joining a cult or exposing themselves to victimisation top of that list. In the main, precarious workers want things that address their problems – always in the top five come help dealing with managers, to know their rights, to earn more.

This can be done informally – by just asking people about their experiences – or formally using anonymous surveys or even action learning sets, described in the next chapter. There is no best option for this – generally people are reluctant to have a first conversation, but it gets easier as you develop a relationship with them. The key is to protect their anonymity and confidentiality and to make that protection clear to people right from the start. Also to keep going back, to seduce people into talking to you if necessary because often the people who need the most help make it the most difficult to do it. Keep trying.

In an emancipatory education framework, the first stage of any activity involves participants defining the issues they are facing, a kind of 'naming' process or problematising about what is going on at work. This is an attempt to engage with people's perceptions of their own situations – and helps them become the subject rather than the object of critical investigation. The facilitator's role is then to ensure that subsequent activities are geared to address the problems as the participants define them. This framework has clear parallels to the psychotherapeutic relationship where sessions are directed by the patient bringing issues, whether consciously or unconsciously, that then determine the focus of the therapeutic work. There is a reason for that awkward silence at the beginning session more than just you having a mean therapist.

It is on the basis of these material needs of people in the workplace that some process of negotiations can start. Do not start your campaign without asking people what they want first. It never works.

Define the battle lines

In order for any organising to work it has to transform individual dissatisfaction into a collective grievance. This means that in order for people to act collectively they have to be clear on the principles they are defending. Successful campaigns have to move quickly from individual grievance to create a collective sense of injustice, including a sense of who is responsible for it. It is only when a campaign is focussed on issues that matter to people – such as fairness – that groups can create a sufficient level of organisation to shape collective demands and action.

In any negotiation the principles behind the demands are important in legitimising the case. Low wages becomes an issue of decent patient care – as in the arguments throughout this book that if you do not treat health workers with respect and provide decent working conditions the state is failing to provide adequate healthcare. The links between patient care and conditions of work has to be continually and forcefully made because it is on the basis of this fundamental principle of the state's duty of care that arguments get won. It is much harder to win a battle over public sector pensions, for example, than it is to win it over the degradation of care that happens when carers themselves become burnt out and vulnerable.

This is a much broader understanding of unionism where the role of unions is to serve human welfare rather than narrow interests such as wage claims or collective bargaining. As work increasingly becomes more precarious and the issues about social justice become much clearer, labour movements have become integrated into broader social movements and work with a wide range of civic and single-issue groups. These societal changes require trade unions to widen their organising model from a simple one of recruiting people into union membership towards an expanded model of building relationships with existing and often spontaneous groups of working people. For trade unions this has become a matter of organisational survival.

Help people understand what is going on

Freire's writing describes two stages of learning: a growing awareness of reality and a commitment to transform that reality. Within this model, learning involves consciousness raising, where we learn about reality including issues of power and oppression through our own experiences and those of the people around us. Emancipatory education takes an ontological position that our perceptions of reality are socially constructed, privileging some versions of reality over others and denying those realities that undermine established realities. As with psychotherapy, emancipatory education is premised on a recognition of reality and bringing into consciousness those aspects of internal and external reality that have been dissociated or denied more broadly at a societal level. The point is not that people are stupid, far from it, but that in groups uncomfortable knowledge gets repressed and hard realities denied.

What is happening now in the UK in relation to joining the dots around inequality is an important example of collective consciousness raising. It used to be the case that if you linked health inequalities with privatisation of services in the NHS you were considered a lunatic. Now it is pretty hard to open a newspaper without the word 'neo-liberalism' popping up. We just see things differently now.

Emancipatory education is fundamentally based on dialogic methods where alternative ideas and perspectives come about through the interaction among people, from which alternative politics can emerge.

Within an emancipatory and psychoanalytic model, consciousness raising at work is predominantly stimulated through dialogue in small groups, providing an important reality-testing function, both at the level of raising consciousness of reality but also developing 'reality-tested relations'. That is, it is through talking to people who do not share the exact same perspective that we are able to test and challenge our own beliefs, making it much more likely that we can see our situation realistically. When you only talk to yourself or people who think the same way as you, your perception of what is going on around you is, well, limited.

Know your rights

One of the strategic advantages of having a union rep at work is that the rep tends to know the law better than human resources (HR). Many workplace conflicts come about because managers did not take the employment relations and law option at university and mistakes will happen. This is not to excuse employers breaking the law, but it does present workers with a strategic advantage that if they do know their rights they are much more likely to be able to defend them.

Legal responsibilities of employers exist, and it is always good to be able to remind them that, for example, employers have a duty to prevent harassment, bullying and discrimination at work and that you are covered against victimisation for raising a complaint.

Things get murky when it comes to raising concerns. In general the advice is to know what your rights and responsibilities are but in the first instance attempt to deal with them informally using the 'soft skills' of persuasion before taking the issue upwards and onwards.

The first and most important stage of raising concerns is to get an objective and detailed picture of the problem. Finding out the who/what/where/when/whys is not a simple process because it will require you collecting factual evidence, checking it and trying to understand it from different perspectives.

Before you raise a concern you need to distinguish between:

* Human error: inadvertent action and mistakes
* At-risk behaviour: actions that are consciously taken that increase risk; these risks are either not recognised or are believed to be acceptable
* Reckless behaviour: where unjustifiable and substantial risk is consciously taken

The nature of the problem should then help you work out what to do next. A collective complaint will be much more powerful than an individual one and may ensure that action is taken more quickly, so if you are concerned about a workplace issue you should speak informally with colleagues you trust first.

The blunt advice is to avoid putting yourself in a situation of whistleblowing – whatever the rights and wrongs of the situation, it is worth raising issues with the people involved first and giving them the chance to resolve them. If you decide to go ahead with whistleblowing, make sure you set up support from the organisations supporting whistleblowers listed in the next chapter.

In the next chapter there are lists for informal meetings and raising concerns. Yes, lists, but if you are actually in the process of raising a complaint chances are you will get stressed, and it is helpful to have a piece of paper that you can check at three in the morning when you are wondering if you are making a huge mistake.

Talk, just talk

The basic principles of emancipatory learning are that all learning starts from the experience of the participants and that we learn new knowledge, attitudes or skills in relation to our life experience. Activities are therefore designed to allow sharing of experiences and ideas – hence the emphasis on talking in small groups and collective problem-solving tasks.

These methods are designed to allow sharing of ideas between people because of the fundamental belief that we learn from people who have the authority of having experienced and survived real problems in life and work. It has the additional benefit that our individual and collective confidence is raised when we recognise that people are capable of solving their own problems.

Within this model dialogue is understood not as a pure form of reflection, or 'verbalism', rather it is mediated by experience of the material world, including emotions and bodily experiences. People talk about how they feel and are encouraged to steer clear of abstractions and intellectualisms. Dialogue here is understood as a process where everyone can present their beliefs but at the same time attempt to remain open to persuasion and respectful of difference. It is not a cynical exercise in patiently listening to someone and then totally ignoring what was said, rather it is taking a position where I am open to what you have said actually influencing my own views. That I am open to you changing my mind.

The skill of the facilitator is key here – to make sure that the discussions are egalitarian, transparent and allow people to say what is on their mind without becoming entrenched. Being skilled at dealing with group dynamics and conflicts, managing the people who speak way too much and those who stay silent, is really handy here. This is not straight forward but works well in smaller groups that feel that the question is authentic and that you are listening to the answer. It also gets easier the more practice you get, and in healthcare settings you have people with incredible communication skills that you can draw on. Find them and use them – personally I have found midwives and mental health nurses to be the most skilled at the stuff of 'difficult conversations'.

Relationality and collective problem solving

Relationality, from a psychoanalytic perspective, is premised on our developmental reliance on our relationships for survival and shaping our identities. In this psychoanalytic model, infant development hinges on our attachments to the people around us. This reliance on our relationships to develop, or grow up, continues throughout adult life, meaning that participation in groups is considered a 'radical arena' for growth and an important vehicle for building collective resourcefulness.

Emancipatory education aims to build agency by increasing decision-making capacity where people can make use of the resources available to them. The final stage of any emancipatory education activity is to plan concrete steps forward. These 'solutions' are based entirely on the experience and ideas of the participants, making use only of the experience within the group. Collective problem solving is based in part on a pragmatic aim to pool ideas and experience, with participants often having enormous experience in dealing with workplace problems. It is also an attempt to build cooperation, linked to psychoanalytic formulations of cohesion in groups established through identification and building social capital. For participants, this involves the commitment to support other members of the group in response to conflicts with employers and the social capital that is generated by this exchange. Collective planning places the responsibility and activity firmly in the hands of the participants and in so doing reinforces their sense of agency and the concrete benefits of collective action.

Emancipatory education methods are highly effective in promoting relationality between participants in part because small groups provide an important 'holding environment' where people can potentially feel secure enough to speak honestly and with authenticity, allowing meaningful relationships to be formed. As a result, being in small groups allows a sense of identification and 'belonging' where people can generalise about their connectedness, but at the same time individuals can maintain their own perspectives. This sense of belonging could be understood as a workplace equivalent of secure attachment, a 'relational security' where a level of trust can be placed in our relationships with others.

Creating containing spaces

Creating the spaces where these conversations can take place is a key part of team building. An idea developed by the psychoanalyst Winnicott and the Tavistock Institute in their work after the Second World War proposes using 'transitional' spaces to help establish authentic communication and relationships. The technique involves establishing temporary small groups and activities where people can feel secure enough to speak honestly, allowing for meaningful relationships to be formed. It is an idea that does not require major organisational buy in, or resources, rather a conscious adoption of participatory methods and some steady holding of the educational frame by the people involved. This means that even in organisations or departments where communication has broken down there is potential for smaller groups and teams to develop effective communication and ways of working.

The model proposed involves setting some ground rules for dialogue and conduct, including respect and confidentiality. Meetings should be regular and facilitated by someone with experience and capacity for managing group dynamics, most likely in a clinical, organisational or educational setting.

This model is similar to clinical and workplace supervisions but takes a more open orientation to content, process and settings. Transitional spaces could include continuing professional development (CPD) workshops or team meetings, social and specialist groups. A common and benign model for a transitional space could be setting up an action learning set; in healthcare these are recognised as important reflective spaces, just a group of people meeting regularly, bringing and sharing work events, experience, feelings and ideas to be worked on with the rest of the group.

On a pragmatic note my experience is that if you ask your workplace for permission to start a new 'project' the answer will pretty much always be no. You do not need permission to set up an informal group or safe space for the people you work with. In fact it is worth having a go at setting up a space informally a few times before going public with what you want to do. Much easier to get people to sign up to something that already exists, and much harder to block it, too.

Future solidarities

One question that preoccupies unions is how to maintain sufficiently strong levels of solidaristic ties between increasingly diverse and insecure groups of workers. In addition to changes in employment relations, this question relates also to societal changes – the decline in cohesive working-class groups and shrinking social-democratic politics. Solidarity understood as an identification between homogenous groups of working people is increasingly not responsive to the diversity of working people's lives. The issue that unions are constantly needing to address is how to build relationships between increasingly insecure and precarious working people sufficient to mobilise collective action.

These are depressing times for anyone interested in collective action at work because we are facing a period of loss and insecurity. However, it is important not to get carried away with the sense of liquid fear that pervades healthcare. Precarity is not happening to the same degree at the same time everywhere; rather, there are still opportunities for people to collectively negotiate better working conditions and relationships. The fact is most of us still have contracts of employment, and unions exist, as do the institutions we need to negotiate with. The system has not totally broken down yet.

Opportunities for negotiations exist predominantly through the large trade unions – Unite and Unison, the Royal College of Nursing (RCN) and BMA. New labour actors, often self-organised, representing precarious workers are also here to stay. The recent high-profile campaigns to secure wages and pro-tections by Deliveroo and Uber workers are good examples of how specific groups of workers come to organise – out of necessity, with the help of some experienced activists, in this case the Independent Workers of Great Britain, legal support from labour friendly solicitors and lots of social media naming and shaming.

These high-profile disputes are incredibly important to understand in terms of the potential and the limitations of carrying out industrial action. The reality is that most precarious workers will not be prepared to act – instead needing a less exposing system of support. One reason online resources, looked at in the next chapter, are so well used is because they offer some degree of anonymity and a first step into scoping out what the problem is and who wants to do anything about it. I am not suggesting that organising is not necessary, it really is, but that with precarious workers strategies have to respect the risks they are willing to take in the process.

Pragmatically speaking, if there is a union in your workplace, join it. If there is an attempt to create a group to look at workplace problems, support it. Give as much time and exposure as you can but no more. The last thing we need in healthcare is another heroic gesture.

However, in a growing number of workplaces unions either do not exist or are weak, and this ironically means that the practices of solidarity are even more important to model and introduce in your workplace. Although it is important to protect yourself at work, just because there is no union does not mean you cannot build solidarity with the people you work with. Far from it. In fact, they are likely to be more receptive to any attempts to show your solidarity.

This might well mean moving from Marx to Freud, moving from an ideological model of solidarity to a relational one. The emphasis shifting from collective organisations to building relationships at work and developing broad negotiating principles and inclusive platforms. This involves a mourning of the loss of a utopian dream of all for one and one for all. At a time when the magic solutions are running out for healthcare workers, we need to play to our strengths, which include a pragmatic insistence that something is better than nothing and a realistic assessment of which issues people can be mobilised to act collectively on.

Solidarity is not a union of like-minded folk who would never hurt each other. Solidarity as an ideal exists precisely because we are all capable of acting defensively and against our own human interests. In a context of insecurity, if there is a fight to be had, it is a psychological one. We must continue to take the risk of practicing solidarity by making contact with other people who are not the same as us. A relational model of solidarity.

Sometimes the very best we can do is just be human amongst other humans, making the best out of a bad lot.

Reading

Cundy L (2015) (Ed) *Love in the Age of the Internet: Attachment in the Digital Era*. London: Karnac.

Ferragina E & Arrigoni A (2016) The rise and fall of social capital: Requiem for a theory? *Political Studies Review* DOI: 10.1177/1478929915623968

Flavin D, Pacek AC & Radcliffe B (2009) Labour unions & life satisfaction: Evidence from new data. *Social Indicator's Research* 98(3):435–444.

Fonagy P, Rost F, Carlyle J, McPherson S, Thomas R, Pasco Fearon RM, Goldberg D & Taylor D (2015) Pragmatic randomized controlled trial of long-term psychoanalytic psychotherapy for treatment-resistant depression: The Tavistock Adult Depression Study (TADS). *World Psychiatry* 14:312–321.

Freire P (1970) *Pedagogy of the Oppressed*. New York: Continuum Books.

French R & Simpson P (2015) *Attention Cooperation Purpose: An Approach to Working in Groups Using Insights from Wilfred Bion*. London: Karnac.

Freud S (1930) Civilization and its discontents. In: Freud S (ed) *Standard Edition*. Vol. 21. London: Hogarth Press, 59–148.

Hoggett P (1992) *Partisans in an Uncertain World: The Psychoanalysis of Engagement*. London: Free Association Books.

Klandermans B (1986) Psychology and trade union participation: Joining, acting, quitting. *Journal of Occupational Psychology* 59:189–204.

McKeown M, Cresswell M & Spandler H (2014) Deeply engaged relationships: Alliances between mental health workers and psychiatric survivors in the UK. In: Burstow B, Diamond S and Lefrancois B (eds) *Psychiatry Disrupted: Theorizing Resistance and Crafting the (R)evolution.* Montreal: McGill – Queen's University Press, 145–162.

Popovic S & Miller M (2015) *Blueprint for Revolution: How to Use Rice Pudding, Lego Men, and Other Non-Violent Techniques to Galvanise Communities, Overthrow Dictators or Simply Change the World.* London: Scribe.

Trade Union Congress (2014) *Your Rights at Work: A TUC Guide,* fourth edition. London: TUC.

Vella J (2002) *Learning to Listen Learning to Teach: The Power of Dialogue in Educating Adults.* San Francisco: Jossey-Bass.

9　Helpful stuff for human beings

"Receiving help is very difficult. There's tremendous ambivalence about recognising we need help. We attack the helper as a way of covering up the shame of needing help."

Despite the hype, nobody is convinced that an app can provide decent healthcare. However, people really do go online to get help, and blogging has become the primary way to share ideas and information about the realities of working life. This is in part because blogging offers the profound-light mix, allowing us to raise deeply troubling issues but with a human touch. The internet allows us to talk about tricky issues using ordinary language, authentically and often hilariously. People respond immediately and positively to other people's experiences in a way that even the best designed workplace wellbeing programme does not offer. The vast majority of people online are not trolls, and in the main human beings respond to other human beings, even when it is done virtually.

This might seem like a less valuable chapter than the others, but for me it is the most important one because it offers some places you can go to get helpful stuff on how to do it. Online technologies are massively important for precarious workers. The technology and its potential anonymity offers a way to find resources without having to go through workplace procedures and is becoming the site of expertise particularly around issues of precarity. By 2014, more people accessed the internet using their smartphones than computers, opening us up to a massive amount of information but with it the occupational hazard of never quite switching off.

Before we go any further we have to be clear about three things. First, always use a personal email account and private social media profiles when you are online. Technically, talking about your employer in anything less than glowing terms could be a breach of your contract. Although most workplaces do not monitor your email, some do, and you cannot assume that monitoring will not take place in the future, particularly if there is conflict at work. It is not an urban myth that people can lose their job for criticising their employer on the work email system or on Facebook. It is always best to keep your employers completely separate from your extracurricular activities, so if you do not have a personal email account, set one up before you go any further.

The same goes for your profile on social media and joining online lists or groups. Always use personal contact details, and never link to your employer's social media or organisational online presence. If you are new to social media, start out using an anonymous profile and then decide about what profile you would like to present online when you have an idea about what you are OK with being seen publicly.

Second, when it comes to online correspondence, posts or comments I still use the advice given to me when I started working in a union – if in doubt, don't send it. Just because someone sends you a message does not mean you have to respond. Written correspondence is always for the record, so keep it short, and if you are not prepared for what you have written to be published in a newspaper, just do not click send. A bit like dating, if you are not prepared to say something to someone's face then you already know they are not that into you.

Third, try to avoid becoming addicted to your smartphone. Most people spend too long online and on their smartphones. Arguably most of this activity involves what we can politely call 'entertainment', but for working people the ability to access our work emails 24/7 is a temptation that many of us fail to manage. Some ground rules about going online involve avoiding these mistakes:

- WRITING IN CAPITALS
- Emailing colleagues at ten at night with 'urgent' updates on project management
- Circumnavigating your existential crisis by checking your messages more than twenty-three times a day
- Looking at Facebook to avoid feelings of loneliness at night – total mistake
- Using a photograph from the 1980s for your online profile
- Texting when it would be better to talk
- Using inspirational quotes about optimism as weapons of mental destruction
- If you are drunk, just step away from the phone

Unless there really is an emergency or you are on call, when it comes to your work email, you just should not go there after eight in the evening. No good will come of it.

Having safely set up your personal email and social media accounts, you could start by looking at the following curated list of resources. These are the sites I use most days – they are reliable and useful and will link you to further resources. The first section gives information about the Surviving Work in Healthcare website set up with the Tavistock and Portman NHS Foundation Trust in 2016. This website offers a series of videos, podcasts and guidebooks designed specifically for health workers. You can download short podcasts and guides onto your smartphone, and it is all absolutely free.

The next section introduces the Surviving Work Library – an archive of anonymous stories of how people survive work. The human voice speaking with honesty and humour is very good for you.

This is followed by a list of campaigning and information sites on healthcare and then some guides on where to get information on discrimination and raising concerns. The final section offers some short introductions on how to raise a concern and setting up an action learning set.

If you have made it to the end of this book the penny will have dropped that surviving work is a long-term process. It is not a survival tick model. There is always a need to return to processes that help us build relationships at work and prepare us for the future workplace realities in healthcare. I hope this book has been helpful in presenting a longer-term framework for you to do precisely that.

Surviving Work in Healthcare

www.survivingworkinhealth.org

Surviving Work in Healthcare is a free resource designed to provide an accessible entry point for key workers and frontline managers to survive work. The resources include a series of conversations between senior practitioners who were brought together to discuss practically how people can survive working in healthcare.

We cover ten themes:

1. **Bullying at work:** Why healthcare has an culture of bullying and why we are all involved
2. **Healthy organisations:** What makes workplaces sick and why we can't stop getting ill
3. **Understanding healthcare:** What are the systemic factors that shape healthcare delivery?
4. **Precarious work:** The realities of working conditions and wages in healthcare
5. **Precarious workers:** What happens to us when we work in precarious jobs
6. **Dynamics in groups:** Why working with other people makes us anxious
7. **Racism:** Why discrimination happens every day in healthcare
8. **Managing healthcare:** How to manage dysfunctional teams and survive the process
9. **Team working:** Why team working is the only show in town
10. **Solidarity in healthcare:** How to make friends and influence people at work

We take a jargon free, de-stigmatizing and practical approach for addressing the real problems of working life, such as how to get on with people at work and dealing with bullying cultures.

The quotes at the beginning of each chapter are taken from the recorded conversations we did with practitioners on these different topics. The videos on the Surviving Work in Healthcare website were recorded in 2015 at the Tavistock and Portman NHS Foundation Trust.

We hope that you can use these resources in your activities, meetings and trainings or just send the link www.survivingworkinhealth.org to anyone you think would find this useful. We want to reach as many people as possible. We do ask that you recognise and respect the copyright of the people involved if you use or disseminate these resources.

If you're working in mental health and you're so tired your eyes are bleeding, settle down with a cuppa and just listen to some short podcasts. You don't have time not to listen.

Surviving Work Library

www.survivingwork.org/library

Say the words 'mental illness' out loud at work and it's like you just farted in a lift. Cue neon sign above your head saying 'run!' and the lift clears in embarrassed silence. Whatever the social no-no's, with a long recession and a global epidemic of despair the gloves are off at work, and we're going to need a few survival skills.

The Surviving Work Library offers free and confidential resources for people who want to actually do it. The library has podcasts and stories from thousands of ordinary experts about how they did it.

We do not promise to make you thinner or richer, but we will help you survive work.

Workplace guides

There are some useful guides we recommend about handling workplace issues:

Zero Tolerance: Dignity at Work, UNITE, http://www.unitetheunion.org/uploaded/docu ments/ZeroToleranceGuide11–18154.pdf

Understanding Grievances and Disciplinaries, TUC, https://www.tuc.org.uk/sites/default/files/ tuc/kyr-understanding-grievances.pdf

Discipline and Grievances at Work: The ACAS Guide, ACAS, http://www.acas.org.uk/media/ pdf/b/l/Discipline-and-grievances-Acas-guide.pdf

Draw the Line: A Managers Guide to Raising Concerns, NHS Employers, http://www.nhsem ployers.org/~/media/Employers/Documents/Campaigns/Draw%20the%20Line/ Draw%20the%20Line%20managers%20guide.pdf

The Duty of Care of Healthcare Professionals, Roger Kline with Shazia Khan, http://www. publicworld.org/files/Duty_of_Care_handbook_April_2013.pdf

Clinical Commissioning Groups and the Workforce Race Equality Standard, Roger Kline and Yvonne Coghill, https://www.england.nhs.uk/wp-content/uploads/2014/10/wres-tech nical-guidance-april-16.pdf

At the time of publication all of these guides are available online for free.

Useful guides about welfare and benefits can be bought from the Child Poverty Action Group at http://www.shop.cpag.org.uk/books.

Health campaign websites

Disabled People Against the Cuts http://dpac.uk.net
Psychologists Against Austerity https://psychagainstausterity.wordpress.com
The Academy of Fabulous NHS Stuff http://www.fabnhsstuff.net
Health Campaigns Together http://healthcampaignstogether.com
Mental Health Task Force https://www.england.nhs.uk/mentalhealth/2016/02/15/fyfv-mh/
NHS Reinstatement Bill Petition 11 March 2016 http://www.nhsbill2015.org
Keep Our NHS Public http://keepournhspublic.com
Big Up the NHS http://www.bigupthenhs.com

Useful practitioner websites

- For analysis of healthcare reform Centre for Health in the Public Interest http://chpi.org.uk
- For information about Balint Groups http://balint.co.uk
- For information on Schwarz Rounds http://www.kingsfund.org.uk/sites/files/kf/field/field_publication_file/schwartz-center-rounds-pilot-evaluation-jun11.pdf
- For research on healthcare The Kings Fund http://www.kingsfund.org.uk
- For good analysis of public policy The London School of Economics' public policy blog http://blogs.lse.ac.uk/politicsandpolicy/
- For blogs about policy from an employment relations perspective the TUC's public policy blog http://touchstoneblog.org.uk
- For an alternative view of economic policy the TUC's economic analysis http://falseeconomy.org.uk

For some support you could try:

- Action for NHS Wellbeing http://www.nhswellbeing.org
- Practitioner Health Programme http://php.nhs.uk
- Big White Wall https://www.bigwhitewall.com

To find your trade unions go to https://worksmart.org.uk/tools/union-finder

The mechanics of raising concerns

The most common concerns in health and social care relate to changes in service delivery such as outsourcing, work intensification, staff shortages and insufficient skills.

In a context of austerity one of the difficult areas for staff is whether to raise concerns over a lack of resources. The professional advice is that if you know there is a serious problem with lack of resources and prioritising them you are obliged to raise your concerns.

For health and social care professionals, the duty of care could mean refusing an instruction where you believe you have been expected to breach your professional code. In this situation, the professional is personally accountable for following his or her professional code and is obliged to refuse instructions on the basis of their duty of care.

Every health and social care professional and manager is responsible for legal duties of care, including professional codes, articulated in the newly amended NHS Constitution. It means that people working in health and social care have a personal duty of care to provide good clinical care and with it a duty of candour to raise concerns about poor practice.

The NHS Constitution sets the principles for how healthcare is delivered. It was amended in 2015 to respond to the Francis inquiries and includes requirements for:

- Patient involvement
- Feedback
- Duty of candour
- Complaints
- Staff rights, responsibilities and commitments
- Dignity, respect and compassion

The NHS Constitution and the Local Authority Social Services and NHS Complaints Regulations 2009 include the obligation for staff to ensure that patients are aware of their rights to make a complaint about their care, including:

- Deadlines for responding to verbal and written complaints
- Offering a discussion about the complaint
- Investigation of any complaint and a written response by the responsible person
- Information about taking the complaint to the CQC and the parliamentary health ombudsman

In 2014 a statutory duty of candour was introduced for all health and social care workers to inform patients when something serious has gone wrong with their care and – even when they do not ask for this information – to try to take action to remedy the problem. Although the duty to raise concerns exists across many regulations and professional standards, the new duty of candour will allow for criminal proceedings against individuals who do not inform patients.

What constitutes a concern?

Your professional code should be the first place you go to for advice on practices in your workplace. Before you raise a concern you need to distinguish between:

- Human error: inadvertent action and mistakes
- At-risk behaviour: actions that are consciously taken that increase risk; these risks are either not recognised or are believed to be acceptable
- Reckless behaviour: where unjustifiable and substantial risk is consciously taken

In order to determine this it may be necessary to talk to the people involved, informally, and encourage them to take other courses of action.

If you are concerned about a workplace issue you should try to speak informally with colleagues about whether they have concerns. A collective complaint will be much more powerful than an individual one and may ensure that action is taken more quickly.

If you have concerns as an individual, take these steps before you start:

- Be clear about your concerns and their level of urgency
- Set out the issues clearly: for yourself, colleagues and managers
- Be clear about the outcomes you are seeking
- Talk to colleagues informally about complaining collectively, either informally or informally
- Request a meeting with the people concerned

If informal contact does not work you will need to raise your concerns with your manager. This should be done carefully to avoid 'blame' and including organisational or contextual factors that may be influencing the practice. You may also want to speak to your union representative – particularly if the issues relate to health and safety concerns, workloads or staff shortages.

The most consistent piece of advice is to try to raise concerns informally either directly with the people concerned or with your direct manager or both. It is advised not to submit a formal concern until other options have been exhausted.

The experience of individual grievance handling is that most concerns are dealt with at the early stages of a grievance procedure where the complainant, often accompanied by a union rep, resolves the issue directly with management.

Good practice shows that raising concerns at a meeting should involve a presentation of the problem – who/what/when/where – how the problem undermines clinical care, relevant policies or professional codes, a statement about what action is needed and if necessary a request for further information. At informal meetings like these it's important to allow managers to respond and also to hold a discussion about the root causes of the problem. Notes should be taken during this meeting and where possible agreement and confirmation on next steps. Sometimes more information and time are needed to work out what action should be taken, but the deadlines for this should be clear. After the meeting you should write an email confirming what was discussed and the outcomes. You should also make sure your own notes are up to date – the details of any discussions are important and easy to forget, particularly if emotions were running high.

Managers' responsibilities

Managers have a responsibility to manage concerns – including having informal meetings and cross-checking concerns against policies and standards. Managers are expected to use a wide range of skills in these processes, including confidentiality, maintaining channels of communication and following formal procedures.

Managers' and NHS board members' responsibilities include:

- Putting in place systems and policies that allow for concerns to be raised and investigated
- Ensuring that staff are not restricted or afraid of raising concerns
- Ensuring that staff understand their duty of candour
- Ensuring that people who raise concerns are not victimised or penalised

List for managers in informal meetings

1   Be nice: remember that whatever is going on, the person you are talking to will have been emotionally affected and probably will be sensitive to how you behave

2   Set the frame: confirm that the discussion is confidential, that you will take notes but these will not be used and that no action will be taken without their consent

3   Listen: just listen to them; don't interrupt them or try to give them an answer, just listen

4   Ask questions: try to establish the core concern and what action needs to be taken

5   Joint planning: agree the way forward with one or more of the following:

   - Keeping a written record of incidents
   - No action to be taken
   - Informal approach to the people concerned

Raising concerns list

- Are you clear what you are concerned about and why? What evidence do you have, and can you get more?
- Does this issue affect you, or can you raise your concerns collectively? If no one else wants to raise your concerns, you should still raise them.
- Have you placed your concerns 'on the record'? Even if you raised them verbally, it is essential that there is an audit trail. Such evidence is essential to protect patients (and yourself).
- Have you set out what you want to achieve? Before you raise your concern, be as clear as you can what you want to achieve.
- It is possible to work together with your employer to address your concerns? It may not be, but if it is, respond positively.
- Check your employer's procedures for raising and escalating concerns.
- Set out in a single statement what your concerns are, the evidence in support, what you want done, when and why.

- If you are offered a meeting do not just turn up for the meeting, prepare for it. Make sure there is a professional, accountable relationship with anyone you invite to represent or accompany you at the meeting such as a trade union rep.

The first and most important stage of raising concerns is to get an objective and detailed picture of what the problem is. Finding out the who/what/where/when/whys is not a simple process because it will require you collecting factual evidence, checking it and trying to understand it from different perspectives.

Given their expertise in handling grievances and legal knowledge we strongly advise you to contact your union rep if you have a union in your workplace. If you need help finding union representation ask colleagues which unions have membership in your workplace – usually this will be the Royal College of Nursing (RCN), the British Medical Association (BMA), Unison or Unite.

If you are unable to resolve the problem locally you are obliged to raise your concerns with someone who has 'sufficient authority' to manage the concerns. Remember that the time limit for submitting a grievance is normally three months and that by far the best strategy is to involve a trade union.

Whistleblowing

Inevitably in cultures where raising concerns is blocked, a greater number of people are forced into whistleblowing. These cases have been high profile over the last five years, and there is a greater understanding that whistleblowing has very poor outcomes both for the whistleblowers and the organisations they come from.

The 'whistleblowing law' – Public Interest Disclosure Act 1998 (PIDA) updated through the 2013 Enterprise and Regulatory Reform Act (ERRA) – covers all staff in the NHS whether directly or indirectly employed. This includes the introduction of redress for workers who suffer from bullying as a result of reporting a concern, meaning that co-workers can be held personally liable for harassing colleagues who raise concerns.

The government also publishes guidance on the prescribed bodies that employees can go to in order to raise their concerns if they are unable to raise issues directly with their employer.

For further advice on whistleblowing we recommend you contact Public Concern at Work, which offers a confidential service. The advice to people considering taking complaints outside of their organisations is to make sure that you have a clear statement of and evidence for your concerns as well as the ability to demonstrate that you have raised your concerns with your employer without success.

Harassment and bullying

Harassment as a form of discrimination is unlawful – enshrined in the Equality Act 2010 – and, although there is no specific legislation against bullying, there are anti-discrimination laws and policies which identify disability, sexuality, religion or belief, class, age, gender and race as potential bases of discrimination. In addition, employers have a legal duty to protect the health, including mental health, and safety of workers whether directly employed or not.

Despite overwhelming opposition, the government repealed the third-party harassment provision under the Enterprise and Regulatory Reform Bill from April 2014. The government said that 'it is unfair that employers should be liable for the actions of third parties over whom they have no direct control'. However, there is protection from third-party harassment from the EU Equal Treatment Directive.

Legal responsibilities of employers:

- Employers have a duty to prevent harassment, bullying and discrimination at work
- You are covered by the anti-discrimination law from day one and even from the day of your interview
- You are covered against victimisation for raising a complaint
- Employees can bring complaints under laws covering discrimination and harassment, health and safety and unfair dismissal
- The 'protected characteristics' in the Equality Act 2010 are gender, pregnancy and maternity, race, disability, sexual orientation, age, gender reassignment, marriage and civil partnership, religion or belief

For a good basic guide on discrimination at work we recommend the TUC's *Your Rights at Work* and the Labour Research Department's *Bullying and Harassment at Work*.

How to protect people who are being bullied:

- The bully is transferred to another section or another department on the same site or to another branch of the organisation
- Until further notice, any attempt by the bully to make direct contact with previous colleagues, other than through an appointed third person, will result in disciplinary measures
- The bully is made fully aware of the effect their behaviour has been having on others
- Human resource managers do not put the bully in a position of managing other employees until his or her behaviours have been addressed

The next step to tackling discrimination could be to put in writing your concerns to the person involved.

Dear _____,

I am writing to complain about what you (did/said) to me (on date/yesterday/this morning) when you _____.

Over the (time period) _____ you have_____.

I want you to stop this behaviour _____.

I find this offensive and unacceptable. I am keeping a copy of this letter, and I shall take further action if you do not stop immediately.

Yours sincerely,

Taking a legal case is generally considered to be the last resort when everything else has failed. There is a nationally set 'three-step' procedure for dealing with dismissal, discipline and grievance issues which must be followed before a legal case can be taken. They are:

* Completing a statement in writing outlining the grounds for grievance
* Carrying out a meeting between the parties involved
* Carrying out an appeal if requested after this meeting

If the grievance process fails you can make a claim to an employment tribunal within a three-month period.

Action learning sets

Action learning sets (ALSs) are a common way for people to establish reflective groups at work. Action learning involves dialogue, reflection and collective problem solving and is consistent with the methods and principles of emancipatory education described in this book. Within healthcare there is some acceptance that these work-focussed groups are legitimate and useful in building patient care and so are a good way to start to establish better relationships at work.

Principles and practices

The groups are set up to run according to a set of principles.

* Confidentiality of the discussions
* Everyone is equal in the group
* Voluntary attendance but commitment to attend regularly

- Commitment made by participants to share their knowledge and experiences and to listen and learn from each other
- Commitment to collective problem solving and planning that comes out of the group

How to organise an action learning set

One of the great things about ALSs is that they can be flexible to their environment. You can run them for one and a half hours to half a day, with normally no more than ten members, approximately once or twice a month. They can be described in any way you think will work in getting people to join – from book clubs to reflective groups, use whatever language you think people will be receptive to. People tend to find it easier to attend a more technical learning set – such as discussing new policy or research – but the reality is however you start the key is to develop a safe and containing space for people to say what they think.

Most new groups will have a regular facilitator with some experience of workplace supervision (such as psychotherapists or other clinicians). However, it depends on the group's experience, and in health settings you often find rotating facilitation.

Meetings normally start with people doing a quick update of where they are. In health settings it is often the case that the group will focus on one critical incident – with a short report and then an open discussion about how to understand it and what can be taken about it. Normally the presenter will listen to the group's reactions and then reflect on what the groups has learned at the end. Groups can set themes, like bullying or racism, and are expected to find collective solutions and actions to take away with them.

Groups do not have to go on forever – they often work for six months, after which the focus can drift. This is not a failure if relationships within the group have been strengthened. The main thing is to keep the energy and pace of the group for as long as people feel it is useful. Groups can also shift in their focus and membership – again, as long as it is responsive to what people actually want, this is a good thing. ALSs work if they are useful, so the key is to respond to the needs that come up rather than to stick to the original plan.

Index